THE CHRIST WHO HEALS

Also by Terryl and Fiona Givens

The God Who Weeps:
How Mormonism Makes Sense of Life

The Crucible of Doubt:
Reflections on the Quest for Faith

THE CHRIST WHO HEALS

HOW GOD RESTORED THE TRUTH THAT SAVES US

FIONA GIVENS
TERRYL GIVENS

DESERET BOOK

Salt Lake City, Utah

© 2017 Fiona Givens and Terryl L. Givens

All rights reserved. No part of this book may be reproduced in any form or by any means without permission in writing from the publisher, Deseret Book Company, at permissions@deseretbook.com or P. O. Box 30178, Salt Lake City, Utah 84130. This work is not an official publication of The Church of Jesus Christ of Latter-day Saints. The views expressed herein are the responsibility of the authors and do not necessarily represent the position of the Church or of Deseret Book Company.

DESERET BOOK is a registered trademark of Deseret Book Company.

Visit us at DeseretBook.com

Library of Congress Cataloging-in-Publication Data
Names: Givens, Fiona, author. | Givens, Terryl, author.
Title: The Christ who heals : how God restored the truth that saves us / Fiona Givens [and] Terryl Givens.
Description: Salt Lake City, Utah : Deseret Book, [2017] | Includes bibliographical references and index.
Identifiers: LCCN 2017040434 | ISBN 9781629723358 (hardbound : alk. paper)
Subjects: LCSH: Plan of salvation (Mormon theology) | Jesus Christ—Mormon interpretations. | Atonement. | Restoration of the gospel (Mormon doctrine) | The Church of Jesus Christ of Latter-day Saints—Doctrines. | Mormon Church—Doctrines.
Classification: LCC BX8643.S25+ | DDC 230/.9332—dc23
LC record available at https://lccn.loc.gov/2017040434

Printed in the United States of America
Publishers Printing, Salt Lake City, UT

10   9   8   7   6   5   4   3   2   1

To Peter

This is the company I should like to find in heaven. Not those flaccid sea anemones of virtue who can hardly wiggle an antenna in the turgid waters of negativity.

—WINSTON CHURCHILL

He . . . healed them that had need of healing.

—LUKE 9:11

Contents

Setting the Stage ix
Introduction 1

PART 1: THE GOSPEL BEFORE THE RESTORATION

Chapter 1: Covenant 11
Chapter 2: God 17
Chapter 3: The Fall 26
Chapter 4: Agency 33
Chapter 5: Sin 37

PART 2: ALL THINGS MADE NEW

Chapter 6: The Selfless Christ 45
Chapter 7: The Adoptive Christ 48
Chapter 8: The Atoning Christ 53
Chapter 9: The Healing Christ 63
Chapter 10: The Collaborative Christ 73
Chapter 11: The Judging Christ 90
Chapter 12: The Saving Christ 103

Epilogue 127
Notes 133
Index 153

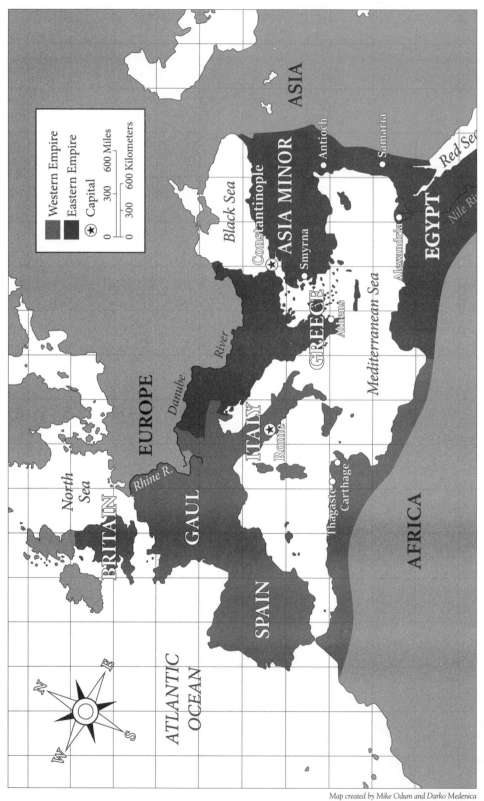

Division of the Roman Empire into Western and Eastern halves, around 285 AD.

Map created by Mike Odum and Darko Medenica

Setting the Stage

By 285 AD the Roman Empire had grown so vast that it was no longer feasible to govern all the provinces from Rome—the capital city. The fifty-first Roman Emperor, Diocletian, therefore divided the empire into halves, with the Western portion governed from Rome and the Eastern governed from Byzantium (later renamed Constantinople after the Emperor Constantine). The division of the Roman Empire into those two halves, as depicted on the map opposite, would later correspond to the formal division of the Western and Eastern Churches in 1054, led from Rome and Constantinople respectively.

The loss of the gospel's "plain and precious" truths[1] was more rapid, and more severe, in the Western Church. In what follows, we will be drawing both parallels and distinctions with several of the Church Fathers—or influential teachers, bishops, and writers of the first Christian centuries. In many cases, with Eastern Fathers in particular, we will see familiar antecedents of Restoration teachings that either survived from the primitive Church or were inspired independent pronouncements. While the Reformation may have ushered in religious diversity and pluralism, its major figures in many cases further deepened the gulf separating Western Christianity from the coming Restoration message.

We include here a "cast of characters" to help readers become more familiar with the lives of some of the men and women whose contributions are vital to an understanding of the healing Christ—the Christ of the Restoration.

SETTING THE STAGE

Cast of Main Characters

Western Fathers

Justin Martyr
(100–165 AD, Samaria)

Born into a pagan family near Jacob's Well, Justin was an avid student of Greek philosophy before his conversion at about the age of thirty. His training prepared him to be one of the Church's first great apologists, defending Christians from false charges and defamation. "Next to God we worship and love the Word, . . . since also He became man for our sakes, that, becoming a partaker of our sufferings, He might also bring us healing."[2] Refusing to sacrifice to idols, he was beheaded with fellow Christians.

Tertullian
(160–220 AD, Carthage)

With Tertullian we find two tragic innovations. He is the first to espouse a doctrine of original sin ("Every soul, then, by reason of its birth, has its nature in [a fallen] Adam until it is born again in Christ; moreover, it is unclean . . . and because unclean, it is actively sinful"); and

Eastern Fathers

Ignatius of Antioch
(ca. 35–ca. 110 AD, modern Turkey)

A bishop of Antioch when a pogrom against Christians was launched in 110 AD, Ignatius was arrested and taken to Rome to be torn apart by wild animals in the arena. A writer of tender letters to early members and Church leaders, Ignatius urged forgiveness, kindness, and unity in the flock. "God appeared in the likeness of man unto newness of everlasting life; and that which had been perfected in the counsels of God began to take effect. Thence all things were perturbed, because the abolishing of death was taken in hand."[6]

Polycarp
(69–156 AD, Asia Minor)

It is reputed that Polycarp, the Bishop of Smyrna (in present-day Turkey), was taught by John the Revelator. According to an early reminiscence, Polycarp "reported his intercourse with S. John and

SETTING THE STAGE

Western Fathers

he is generally understood to take a position against philosophy and rationality in general as applied to religion ("what has Athens to do with Jerusalem?"; and "it is by all means to be believed because it is absurd [*ineptum*]")³. He parted ways with the institutional Church when he opted to support a movement (the Montanists) that affirmed the gift of continuing prophecy.

Augustine
(354–430 AD, Thagaste [modern Algeria])

Augustine had one of the most dramatic conversions in Christian history, which he wrote about in his masterful *Confessions*. He became a bishop, an enormously prolific writer, and one of the primary shapers, after Paul, of the Christian tradition—at least in the West. He initially supported the doctrine of preexistence, but changed his position later in life. And he initially defended freedom of the will, but ultimately decided it was incompatible with his defense of grace. His embrace of original sin entrenched the doctrine firmly in

Eastern Fathers

the rest of the apostles who had seen the Lord, and how he used to mention their words, and what the things were that he had heard from them."⁷ He died heroically at the stake, according to witnesses. Asked to repudiate Christ, he said, "How can I blaspheme my king who has saved me?"⁸

Irenaeus
(130–202 AD, Asia Minor)

Irenaeus was one of the earliest expounders of the Christian faith, and he wrote with authority. He remembered with awe the days in which he sat "in the place where . . . Polycarp used to sit and discourse," and how he "listened eagerly" to the disciple of John and made notes of what he heard, "not on paper, but in my heart."⁹ In the writings of Irenaeus, we hear some of the purest and most undiluted doctrines as taught by Jesus and his apostles. "Our Lord Jesus Christ, the Word of God, of his boundless love became what we are that he might make us what he himself is."¹⁰

SETTING THE STAGE

WESTERN FATHERS

Western Christianity. He could write movingly about the innate yearning of all for the Divine Presence: "our heart is restless until it repose in thee."[4]

Pelagius
(360–418 AD, Britain?)

Little is known about this British monk, except that he was a highly influential writer. Upon his arrival in Rome he took a strong stand against Church teachings on original sin, infant baptism, and predestination, preaching that free will as well as grace was necessary for salvation. "The man who hastens to the Lord, and desires to be directed by him, that is, makes his own will depend upon God's . . . does all this by the freedom of the will."[5] Unsurprisingly, he incurred the wrath of Augustine and the condemnation of a Church council in 418 AD.

EASTERN FATHERS

Clement of Alexandria
(150–215 AD, Athens)

This Father promoted two principles that would be more fully elaborated in modern scripture: first, preexistence, and second, our destiny as full heirs with Christ. Regarding the first, he wrote that "the ancient and universal church . . . collect[s] as it does into the unity of the one faith . . . those already ordained, . . . God . . . knowing before the foundation of the world that they would be righteous."[11] As for exaltation, he said, "The Word of God became man, that thou mayest learn from man how man may become God."[12]

Origen
(185–254 AD, Alexandria)

The extraordinarily prolific Origen would have been martyred as a boy alongside his father had his mother not exploited his modesty by hiding his clothes, preventing him from rushing out the door to be killed with his father. After his father's death, he supported his family through his teaching and writing, and he later composed the first systematic treatise on

SETTING THE STAGE

Eastern Fathers

the Christian faith. He championed the preexistence of human spirits and took literally our joint-heirship with Christ: "The Son in his kindness generously imparted deification to others ... who are transformed through him into gods, as *images* of the prototype."[13] Though initially considered one of the greatest theologians and Father of the Church, both those teachings associated with his name were anathematized in the sixth century.

Macrina
(324–379 AD, Asia Minor)
Macrina belonged to one of the most influential of early Church families, was esteemed as an example of holiness and devotion, and possessed the gift of healing. She influenced her brother Gregory of Nyssa so profoundly that he called her "teacher." Another brother, Basil, was a pioneer of the monastic tradition, following her example in founding and leading the first Christian monastery. She believed all would eventually be drawn to accept Christ, and taught that "the principle of

SETTING THE STAGE
EASTERN FATHERS

anger cannot be found in God." The soul is drawn to the Good "by means of the movement and activity of Love."[14]

Gregory of Nazianzus
(329–390 AD, Asia Minor)

Born in Asia Minor (now Turkey) to Christian parents, Gregory inclined to solitude and study (he edited the important writings of Origen, among other works). Pressured to accept ordination, he relented and eventually held the office of Archbishop of Constantinople. Still, we see in Gregory a simple and moving devotion to the Savior that reverberates through the centuries:

"I am filled with indignation and grief for my Christ (and I would that you might sympathize with me) when I see my Christ dishonoured on this account on which He most merited honour."[15]

Gregory of Nyssa
(ca. 335–ca. 394 AD, Asia Minor)

Brother of Macrina, Gregory was renowned and loved for his gentle character. Unlike so many who tended toward asceticism

SETTING THE STAGE
EASTERN FATHERS

and self-loathing, Gregory celebrated human nature and potential, believing that no punishment would be eternal and that God's forgiveness was so complete it would extend to all men, even the fallen Lucifer. Human souls, he wrote, will eventually be "like celestial palm groves," having acquired the divine nature and become deified. Why did God create humans? Because no "aspect of the divine nature should remain idle with no one to share it."[16]

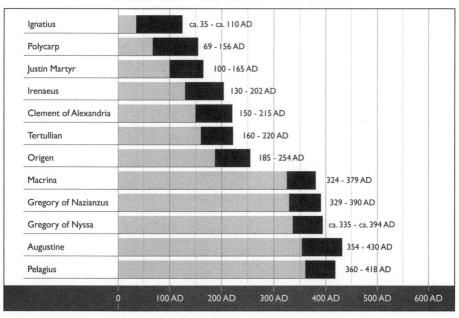

Church Fathers Timeline

SETTING THE STAGE

Western Reformers

Martin Luther
(1483–1546 AD, Germany)

After a near miss from a lightning strike, Martin Luther took orders as an Augustinian monk in 1505 AD. Fearing God's wrath and feeling incapable of earning salvation through obedience, Luther developed Augustine's ideas into the doctrine of salvation by grace alone through faith in Christ, denying both free will and any inherent human capacity for good. ("Faith is a living, daring confidence in God's grace."[17]) He also reduced Church sacraments from seven to two (baptism and Eucharist) and redefined them as signs rather than channels of grace. These doctrines, and his attacks on the corruptions of the Catholic Church, launched the Reformation.

John Calvin
(1509–1564 AD, France)

Exposed to Luther's writings as a young man, Calvin broke with Catholicism and developed his own theology, differing from Luther on the meaning of the Eucharist and other doctrines. In addition to embracing salvation by grace alone, Calvin emphasized human bondage to sin, election (predestination), and God's absolute sovereignty ("Nothing takes place by chance; everything is governed by God's hand."[18]). Presbyterians, Congregationalists, Methodists, Baptists, and Quakers—all were shaped to varying degrees by Calvinist thought.

Miscellaneous Inspired Voices

Julian of Norwich
(1342–1416 AD, England)

During a near-fatal illness as a young woman, Julian experienced a series of visions. She spent twenty years as an anchorite, meditating in solitude on the meaning of those revelations. Writing about these "showings" and her hard-won insight into the universal reach of God's absolute love, she became one of the most revered religious figures of the Middle Ages. "Full preciously our good Lord keepeth us when it seemeth that we be cast away for our sin. . . . I was greatly astonished by this wonder and marvel, that he who is so to be revered and feared would be so familiar."[19]

Edward Beecher
(1803–1895 AD, America)

A member of the most prominent religious family in America, Edward was brother to Harriet Beecher Stowe and Henry Ward Beecher, and son of Lyman Beecher. As a young man he had a moving vision of the preexistence, which doctrine he defended in a major work entitled *Conflict of Ages*. He also wrote a passionate repudiation of the sovereign God taught in his Calvinist tradition, arguing instead for a Heavenly Father moved by the suffering of His children. Beecher's nonconformity cost him the success and fame that otherwise would have been his. He said, "Of all errors, none are so fundamental and so wide reaching in their evil tendencies and results as errors with respect to the character of God."[20]

Nikolai Berdyaev
(1874–1948 AD, Ukraine)

A convert from Marxism to Christianity, he was exiled to Siberia for his religious ideas and then expelled from the Soviet Union for his political ideas. He saw in the Orthodox tradition the best hope for a view that accorded to humankind both dignity and freedom, because "it did not define man from the point of view of Divine justice but from the idea of transfiguration and Deification of man and cosmos."[21] Initially excommunicated by his church, he felt nonetheless that this faith tradition came closest to promising the universal salvation he believed God would offer His children. Today he is one of the most revered theologians of the Orthodox tradition.

Introduction

He hath sent me to heal the brokenhearted, to preach deliverance to the captives, and recovering of sight to the blind, to set at liberty them that are bruised.

—LUKE 4:18

It is our thesis in writing this book that to be a Latter-day Saint is to embrace a particular understanding of Christ. While our confirmation formalizes our membership in an institutional Church, it is through our baptism that we are adopted into a divine family, assuming Christ's name. It is a Christ, we hope to show, who comes into his full splendor and beauty through the lens of the Restoration. Mormonism is so rich in doctrine, so expansive in its teachings, that we may be too easily distracted from this one cardinal proposition: The Restoration recovered that Christ who is the most remarkable being in the history of religious thought. As an early Church Father, Tertullian, wrote, Christ "reforms our birth by a new birth from heaven; he restores our flesh from all that afflicts it; he cleanses it when leprous, gives it new light when blind, new strength when paralyzed, . . . when dead he raises [us] to life."[1]

Finding shared ground with fellow Christians is a valuable enterprise. Restoration scriptures teach repeatedly of a universal Church comprising all those who "come unto Christ," including "holy men" and women Joseph "[knew] not of," a community culled from all ages and cultures.[2] Those same scriptures admonish us to seek after the truth in "all good books, . . . languages, tongues, and people," as well as in scriptural records not belonging to the standard works, such as the Apocrypha.[3] The Restoration scriptures encourage us as individuals and as a Church community to seek after good everywhere and make it a part of our religion. "The grand fundamental principle of Mormonism is to receive truth let it come from where it may."[4] As the Prophet Joseph Smith stated: If the Methodists, Presbyterians, or others have any truth, then we should embrace it. One must "get all the good in the world" if one wants to "come out a pure Mormon."[5]

We are in awe of the discipleship manifest across the religious spectrum of the world. We admire the moral fervor of Martin Luther, the piety of John Wesley, and the benevolence of Quakerism's founder, George Fox. We feel holy envy of the liturgical beauty and power of the mass. We love the theological richness of contemporary Anglican writers and relish the devotional earnestness of the Eastern Church Fathers, who followed in the footsteps of the apostles. Together with millions of fellow Christians we celebrate a shared belief in the divinity of Jesus Christ and in the efficacy of his Atonement. However, in this book, we would like to emphasize how the doctrines and scriptures of the Restoration have enriched our knowledge of the rock and foundation of our faith—Jesus Christ.

Mormonism has immense theological profundity. It repudiates notions of inherited guilt and depravity, restores vulnerable compassion and empathy to a Heavenly Father, recaptures the saga of human preexistence and our literal co-heirship with Christ, and provides a coherent scheme of salvational plenitude for the dead as well as the living. Its doctrines are alternately exhilarating and consoling, controversial and common-sensical. However, in our emphasis on the particularities of the Restoration—a boy prophet, gold plates, seer stones, and restored priesthood—we too often pass over our faith in Christ, thinking of it as a commonly shared Christian

INTRODUCTION

belief that deserves little more comment. A missionary church has an imperative to build bridges and find common ground. However, if the Restoration recuperates nothing truly revolutionary, crucially different, distinctively and uniquely salvific about Jesus the Christ, then the entire enterprise adds little more than some marginalia and footnotes to the Christian plan of salvation. A wholesale restoration would not be needed if nineteenth-century Christology had not been lacking plain and precious truths. We believe it was. The Lord's message to Joseph in the grove, using disturbingly stark language, was that certain crucial, creedal declarations about Christian fundamentals were devastatingly, destructively wrong. This was not an indictment of the millions of humble seekers of God throughout Christendom, but of those historical declarations that have obscured, misrepresented, and impaired our access to the true and living Christ. For this reason, we believe that no religious contribution of Joseph Smith could possibly transcend in significance a restored knowledge of the true nature and character and conduct of God the Father, and especially the Son, the Savior of the world. Our emphasis in this small volume, therefore, will be on ascertaining how a Latter-day Saint, relying upon the truths the Restoration assembled, might find a fuller and richer response to the question posed by Christ: "But whom say ye that I am?"[6]

It may be helpful, in this regard, to chart briefly the *prehistory* of the beginning of God's Restoration through his prophet Joseph Smith Jr. In the first section to follow, we trace some of the major currents of Christian understanding as they took conflicting shape among the first generations of Christians and were dramatically refashioned in the centuries following Augustine, culminating in the Protestant Reformation. This review is essential not just to set the stage historically; it is our suggestion that we Latter-day Saints are still too reliant upon the assumptions, the implications, and especially the language that generations of well-intentioned but misguided theologians and Reformers alike introduced into the domain of religious thought. We wish to focus on language in particular because language is one of the most subtle yet critically important ways in which erroneous understandings, harmful assumptions, and self-defeating paradigms and labels insinuate themselves into our habits of thought and therefore action. Latter-day Saints' understanding of the gospel, God's revelations to prophets and members, church worship and temple ritual—all are mediated by language. Both Joseph Smith and holy writ warn us about the limitations of language to capture the mind and will of God adequately and the truth fully and effectively. Perhaps renewed attention to, and careful assessment of, the language we have inherited uncritically from previous traditions might be helpful.

The Problem of Language

Latter-day Saints take seriously the story of Adam and Eve[7] as the progenitors of humanity with whom Jesus Christ communed in person. Initially, language does not appear to have been a problem. "And a book of remembrance was kept," we read in Moses, "the which was recorded, in the language of Adam, for it was given unto as many as called upon God to write by the spirit of inspiration, . . . [in] a language which was pure and undefiled."[8] Things had changed considerably by the time of Christ's coming. Even among his New World disciples, when God spoke from heaven, the voice was not recognized. When Christ appeared at the temple in Bountiful, the assembled throng heard "a voice as if it came out of heaven; . . . a small voice [that pierced] them that did hear to the center, . . . and they cast their eyes round about, for they understood not the voice which they heard."[9] When Jesus knelt shortly thereafter and prayed with his people, it is recorded that "the things which he prayed cannot be written," neither could any "tongue . . . speak" the words he uttered.[10]

During the early stages of the Restoration, when Joseph tried to convey his spiritual promptings and inspired insights into published revelations, he sought the help of half a dozen other men. Together, they worked and edited and revised, attempting to capture more adequately the glimmers of revealed truth.[11] Joseph mourned the difficulty of the enterprise: "Oh Lord God deliver us in thy due time from the little narrow prison almost as it were total darkness of paper pen and ink and a crooked broken scattered and imperfect language."[12]

The Lord himself acknowledged the daunting challenges at our end of the communication line, assuring us that "these commandments are of me, and were given unto my servants *in their weakness*, after the manner of *their* language."[13] Brigham Young elaborated the principle: "When God speaks to the people, he does it in a manner to suit their circumstances and capacities. . . . Should the Lord Almighty send an angel to re-write the Bible, it would in many places be very different from what it now is. And I will even venture to say that if the Book of Mormon were now to be re-written, in many instances it would materially differ from the present translation. According as people are willing to receive the things of God, so the heavens send forth their blessings."[14]

When one adds to the challenges of our own limitations the loss of "plain and precious things,"[15] the unintentional errors of well-intentioned scribes, together with the culturally conditioned concepts and language of generations of copyists and translators, it is understandable why Joseph would say "Many things in the bible . . . do not, as they now stand, accord with the revelation of the holy Ghost to me."[16] For all these reasons, the terrain becomes subtly but pervasively strewn with "traditions of the fathers." It is no wonder that even restored truth has a hard time flourishing amidst the weedy plot of ground that we have inherited. Joseph himself understood that the difficulty was more than linguistic; we inherit a conceptual vocabulary as well, full of unchallenged assumptions and concepts. He stated, "There has been a great difficulty in getting anything into the heads of this generation it has been like splitting hemlock knots with a corn dodger for a wedge & a pumpkin for a beetle. Even the Saints are slow to understand. I have tried for a number of years to get the minds of the Saints prepared to receive the things of God, but we frequently see some of them after suffering all they have for the work of God will fly to pieces like glass as soon as any thing comes that is contrary to their traditions."[17]

In the following pages we wish to review how centuries of Christian tradition have shaped our understanding of key terms and concepts in ways that are not consistent with the gospel as Christ taught it and as it was restored through Joseph. Unprepared, we might recoil at the harshness of the language Joseph heard in the grove, referring to Christian creeds of his day as "an abomination"[18]; clearly, the Lord knew the religious world we have inherited from well-meaning Reformers is rife with teachings, assumptions, doctrines, and dogmas that take us further away, rather than closer to, the gospel Christ taught. Some have argued that it is not what we believe that matters, but what we do, that true principles matter less than right action. Certainly there is some validity in such a claim. However, what we believe *does* matter. "If our beliefs do not influence our daily decisions—our religion is vain, and our faith, if not dead, is certainly not well and is in danger of eventually flat-lining," confirmed President Dieter F. Uchtdorf.[19]

What we believe about God and his Christ—their nature, their attributes, their character—shapes our response to the Heavenly Family and their designs for us. Arguments about the cosmological location of Kolob will not advance our salvation. Ascertaining the true depth and extent of God's love, however, will. "Of all errors," wrote the great and unorthodox nineteenth-century Congregationalist minister Edward Beecher, "none are so fundamental and so wide reaching in their evil tendencies and results as errors with respect to the character of God."[20] Only an accurate understanding of God's "character, perfections, and attributes" can effect the necessary transformation of our wounded state to immortal glory.[21] Correct language is part of that correct understanding.

We fear we may not be aware enough, vigilant enough, informed enough, about the harm unleashed, the truths disfigured, and the

INTRODUCTION

healing confounded because a fallen language has intervened between our Heavenly Parents' original benevolent purposes and our contemporary understanding of key Christian themes. Only a vocabulary with the capacity to capture eternal truth has the transcendent power to comfort, console, and transform us.

In Part 1 that follows, we trace some of the major changes that were introduced into the Christian narrative, reshaping our conceptions about God, the Fall, human nature, sin, and—most important for our present purposes—the role of our Redeemer. Before we can begin to know and appreciate Christ in his saving power as Healer, we need to be able to identify the major moments of divergence from the great plan of happiness as it was originally expounded in heaven and reinstituted in the final dispensation. We believe that recognizing these innovations, and their detrimental effects on the language we use in our self-understanding and in our thinking about our own spiritual journeys, can be a useful and healthy corrective. Our hope is that, as we illustrate in Part 2, on such a foundation we might more joyfully appreciate the power and sweep of Restoration teachings about Christ and know that in this dispensation, indeed, "all things are become new."[22]

PART 1

THE GOSPEL BEFORE THE RESTORATION

The great plan of happiness incorporated several key elements clearly taught and understood in the Christian Church's formative years. All underwent revision and alteration in subsequent centuries—especially in Western Christianity, with its headquarters in Rome, which followed Augustine's theology of the centrality of sin and consequent human depravity. The Eastern Christian tradition, with its base in Constantinople, maintained a course much more in harmony with LDS conceptions of the gospel, and LDS doctrine tracks more closely with the Eastern Church Fathers than it does with the Roman Catholic Church in the West and its Protestant offshoots.

Remnants and traces of the eternal gospel are discernible in the records left us from those first centuries, as are key moments of transition and loss. Joseph Smith, in bringing the Church "out of the wilderness," recognized, as did his fellow laborers in the Restoration, that the original Church, "once indeed beautiful, pure, and intelligent;—clothed with the power and spirit of God," by 1830 "lay . . . in broken fragments scattered, rent, and disjointed; with nothing to point out its original, [except] the shattered remnants of its ancient glory."[1] Abundant traces of the eternal gospel were still discernible, however, as dispersed "fragments of Mormonism."[2] With the "ancient palace" now reduced to ruins, the work of restoration would entail bringing together the new and the old, the excavation and assemblage of what was sound and the replacement and incorporation of what had been irredeemably lost or corrupted even before Christ's ministry. In the records of some early Christian Fathers we are able to recognize elements of the pure gospel restored through Joseph. With these early Christian writers, we can trace this original gospel narrative back in time beyond the primitive Church, even beyond Eden, to premortal worlds, where the story begins.

CHAPTER 1

Covenant

FROM ETERNAL TO REMEDIAL

*[The King and the Queen] made a covenant with me
and wrote it in my heart so I would not forget.*

—SONG OF THE PEARL[1]

Within the eternal sweep of the gospel narrative, we find that grace did not enter the universe with the setting of the cross upon a hill in Calvary. Grace entered the universe when, ages before the earth was formed or the first rainbow appeared, "we [became] part of a divine plan designed by Heavenly Parents who love us."[2] On that occasion, a proposal was presented to an assembled multitude.[3] From "the midst of spirits and glory," and being greater than them all, said Joseph, God "saw proper to institute laws whereby the rest, who were less in intelligence, could have a privilege to advance like Himself and be exalted with him."[4] Such exaltation entails the uniting of all of us in the familial pattern found in heaven. As Elder Erastus Snow declared, "There never was a God, and there never will be in all eternities, except they are made of these two component parts; a man and a woman; the male and the female."[5] Or, as the Church recently reaffirmed, quoting a First Presidency statement, to be "in the similitude of the universal Father and Mother" means we are "the sons and daughters of Deity."⁶ In those premortal councils, God presented a comprehensive blueprint for the constituting of a glorious Heavenly Family, sealed by the Holy Spirit of Promise into richer and more abundant relationships than those then enjoyed. Supernal grace was manifest a second time when, in response to God's question, "Whom shall I send?," Christ presented himself as the costly offering through which the entire human family could thus be united in an immortal and eternal life with our Heavenly Father and Heavenly Mother.

Recognizing that a permanent binding together of the human family could occur, our Heavenly Parents clarified precepts and instituted ordinances, along with a mortal educative process, for the purpose of establishing and eternalizing an endless web of familial relationships. We understand the earth to have been created for this very purpose: to place the human family into eternal order. Marriage was ordained and families established "that the earth might answer the end of its creation; and that it might be filled with the measure of man, according to his creation before the world was made."⁷

Thus, an eternal covenant was confirmed, one that would be etched in our hearts as in God's and that would form the backbone of an enduring relationality to be preserved, enhanced, and solidified through eons of earthly history and beyond. Versions of this understanding of an everlasting covenant made in heavenly courts before earth's creation survived in some Jewish understanding and the Jewish culture out of which Christianity arose. It was one of the key tenets of a primordial gospel that those chosen people preserved and taught. "The idea of a covenant between a deity and a people is unknown from other religions and cultures," notes the *Encyclopedia Judaica*.⁸ In some Jewish traditions, the righteous souls were "called together by God before He created the universe."⁹ Traces of this original understanding persisted in Jewish thought for some time. "All the souls which existed from Adam onward," wrote Menasseh ben Israel in the seventeenth century, "were all in the garden of Eden."¹⁰

He added that these preexistent souls were all present at Sinai and participated in the reaffirmation of the covenant. This last assertion he found attested by the verse in Deuteronomy 29:14, "I make this covenant to those who are standing here, and with those who are not here with us today."[11] Jewish conceptions of preexistence persisted beyond the early Christian world, and traditions of a populous heavenly assembly, "the council of Yahweh," continued on into the rabbinic era.[12]

Such views are not universal within Judaism; Jon Levenson, for instance, writes that Israel "was called into existence at a moment in ordinary time and at a specifiable place"[13] and insists that Israel's "identity is not cosmic and primordial."[14] Mormons hold it is both. Early Christians agreed. Origen, the first systematic theologian the primitive Church produced, wrote in the early third century that we began in God's presence as spiritual children, and that we are sent into a world "full of struggles and trials." God will persevere with us, he taught, as we advance through this world and the next. "Improved by this . . . method of training," he believed, and instructed by the angels there, we will "advance . . . through each stage to a better condition" until we "reach even to that which is invisible and eternal."[15]

Mormons believe that all those born into the world chose to enter into the everlasting covenant in that great council, where we along with Abraham were promised "an earth whereon [to] dwell," a probationary "second estate," and "glory added upon [our] heads for ever and ever."[16] As Joseph taught, "the organization of the spiritual and heavenly worlds, and of spiritual and heavenly beings, was . . . voluntarily subscribed to by themselves."[17] The daunting process deterred many, who were dissuaded by what Robert Frost called the "sacrifice of those who for some good discerned . . . gladly g[a]ve up paradise." Those of us who assumed mortality, however, did so "by assenting voice," for "none are taken but who will."[18] The early Christian text composed during the New Testament era, the *Song of the Pearl*, alluded to above, beautifully renders this making of the eternal covenant in allegorical form. This narrative describes Heavenly Parents who

> *sent me on a mission*
> *from our home in the east. . . .*
> *They took off my bright robe of glory,*
> *which they had made for me out of love,*
> *and took away my purple toga,*
> *which was woven to fit my stature.*
> *They made a covenant with me*
> *and wrote it in my heart so I would not forget.*[19]

Through historical processes and human fallibility, the larger cosmic context for this project was lost (after Christ's death, but recurrently in prior ages as well). Despite the surviving fragments of the whole in Church Fathers such as Origen and Irenaeus, the overall conception was lost. Hence, imperfect humans and their institutions reconfigured the covenant in a tragically attenuated form of limited prehistory, extent, and impact. This "falling away" does not represent some minor corruptions of sacramental liturgy or ritual forms. It is not about wicked priests whom God punished by removing their priesthood. It is about a fundamental misapprehension of the background and purpose and extent of the covenant (premortal origins, mortal incarnation, and eventual theosis and sealing into the eternal family). It is the loss of the mode by which that covenant is executed (through temple covenants that create those chains of infinite belonging, completing our journey from intelligence to joint heirship with Christ).

The loss of the larger cosmic context was compounded by failing to see the Fall as a necessary and premeditated immersion of humankind into the crucible of experience, suffering, and schooling in the practice of love. The loss was not about baptizing at the wrong age or in the wrong medium. It was about not knowing that baptism makes us—all of us eventually—literally members of Christ's family and co-heirs with him as planned in premortal councils. What is at stake is not simple difference in standards of sexual practice or marriage's purpose per se. It is about failing to see the family structure as a divine mode of eternal association that is at the very heart of heaven itself. In sum, the "Restoration" is not about *correcting* particular doctrines or practices as much as it is about *restoring* their cosmic context. Consequently, Mormon emphasis on proper priestly administrators is not about authority for authority's sake. It is about officiators who understand the contextual origins of that authority and the purposes for which priestly authority is to be used. It is about the performance of those sacred sacraments under God's immediate direction, according to God's original intentions and designs. In Joseph's understanding, the tragedy that befell Christendom resulted from a critically impoverished account of the everlasting covenant, one that rendered all sacraments and ordinances ineffectual not through wickedness but through lost understanding of their scope and purpose—namely, to constitute the human family into a durable, eternal, heavenly association.

Fragmented memories of that heavenly prelude to our earthly life appear in the world's most ancient religions and belief systems. Mesopotamian creation narratives, Greek myths and philosophy, and early Jewish texts all make reference to a life in the spirit before embodiment. Besides Origen, early Christian writers like pseudo-Clement, Clement of Alexandria, Evagrius, and even the young Augustine all affirmed and defended the teaching. However, this core doctrine was abandoned over time due to fear of impinging upon God's presumed sovereignty, a distrust of related Gnostic teachings, Augustine's change of heart, and the Church's condemnation of Origen and his teachings. By the sixth century, the doctrine of human preexistence had been declared anathema and had virtually disappeared from Christian tradition.

With the Garden rather than heavenly courts thought to be Adam's first abode, traditional Christianity starts the covenant in

Eden. With no premortal context to give Eve's choice its due honor, Christians could only read that choice as fatally wrong. Even the possibility of the wisdom Eve revealed in her tribute to mortality was no longer conceivable. ("Were it not for our transgression we never should have had seed, and never should have known good and evil, and the joy of our redemption, and the eternal life which God giveth unto all the obedient.")[20] Eve's Ode to Joy reflects God's pleasure with her decision to privilege dynamic growth over stasis, costly life and death over undiscovered potentiality. "[They have] become as one of us," speak the gods, "to know [that is, to experience] good and evil," pleasure and pain.[21]

The progenitors of the human race, who "fell that men might be," become increasingly reduced to the guilty pair who bring upon their descendants "all our woe, with loss of Eden."[22] In the place of the eternal covenant founded in heavenly councils and unfolding still, Christianity substitutes the doctrine of an Adamic covenant—the "covenant of works"—initiated in the Garden, which ends in disaster. In the aftermath of Adam's failure to fulfill his obligation of perfect obedience, God makes provision for a new covenant—a covenant of grace, which comes into being only with Christ's atoning sacrifice. In this context, the plan of salvation becomes triage for a plan that has failed. "God's purpose and goal in redemption," writes one religious historian, "is to reverse the sin, corruption and death introduced into humanity by Adam."[23] For the unfailing plan initiated in heavenly councils that foresaw a necessary immersion in mortal experience, a Christianity stripped of premortal existence becomes instead a story that is primarily about recuperation, repair, and rehabilitation. The loss of this truth about pre-earthly councils and covenants acted as a falling domino that set in motion an entire series of catastrophic changes to the Christian understanding of God, humans, and Christ's role in our redemption.

CHAPTER 2

GOD

FROM PARENT TO SOVEREIGN

The church fathers . . . say hardly anything about the tenderness of God, not because the subject was unknown to them, but more because of their true sense of godly reserve.

—DANIEL BOURGUET[1]

An early casualty of the confluence of two factors—Greek philosophy that disparaged materiality and Jewish monotheism that embraced only one divine being—was the absorption of Christ the divine into Trinitarian models. Some Church Fathers, like Justin Martyr, saw the divinity of Christ as clear evidence that there were two Gods worshipped by Christians. The God who appeared to Abraham and Moses, he wrote, was "another God and Lord."[2] In this way, he and other Christians understood—in terms remarkably familiar to Latter-day Saints—that "the name 'god' need not be restricted to the supreme deity. Jesus . . . might be described as a god, but in such a way that one could speak of two gods."[3]

Opponents of early Christianity as well recognized that Christians were worshipping two deities. It was difficult to refute the charge of the pagan Celsus, who fumed that "if the Christians worshipped only one God they might have reason on their side. But as a matter of fact they worship a man who appeared only recently. They do not consider what they are doing a breach of monotheism, rather they think it perfectly consistent to worship the great God and to worship his servant as God."[4]

This conception of two separate Gods was clearly the norm. In fact, scholars recognize "how deeply the conception of a plurality of divine Persons was imprinted on the apostolic tradition and the popular faith."[5] Origen stated the case simply: "We worship, then, the Father of truth, and the Son who is the truth. And they are two separate persons, but one in unity and concord of mind."[6]

What Celsus draws attention to, however, is that at this early date, Christians were under urgent pressure to define themselves as monotheists, to differentiate themselves from the polytheists by whom they were surrounded, to rebut criticism, and to avoid persecution at the hands of oppressors such as Emperor Marcus Aurelius Augustus. In a remarkably frank assessment of motive, Roger Olson writes that "Christians were faced with a choice: either ignore Celsus and critics like him and retreat into a folk religion without intellectual defense or rise to the challenge and develop cogent doctrines that would reconcile [the] . . . contradictory belief such as monotheism and the deity of Jesus Christ."[7] Christians, therefore, developed Trinitarian ideas to remain within the monotheistic fold—even though early Christians like the *Shepherd of Hermas* (a first- or second-century Christian text) and Justin Martyr plainly described God and Christ as separate and distinct Deities. Of their views, however, a Christian historian says—without the least hint of irony—that if we hope to find insight with writers so close in time to Jesus we are "expecting far too much from a second-century church father."[8]

A second great casualty in the early Christian period, in addition to Christ's separate and distinct divinity, was the literal fatherhood of God with all that implied. The earliest Christian "General Handbook of Instructions," the first century *Didache*, encouraged Christians to employ the Lord's Prayer several times daily. One historian notes a beautiful insight that such love for that prayer invites: Christians, following the example of the Savior, are the first to address God as Father. "To do so is a distinctive mark of the disciples of Jesus who, through him, are sons and daughters of God."[9] Jesus was clear and emphatic in urging his disciples to enter into filial relationship with God. Paul testified to the Romans that we "have received the Spirit of adoption, whereby we cry, Abba, Father."[10] "My Father, and your Father," Jesus told Mary.[11] Latter-day Saints hold that the familial relationship into which we are invited as eternal members is the very essence of the everlasting covenant enshrined in the premortal councils of heaven.

Christianity, however, soon veered sharply away from the parent-child relationship articulated by Christ in the New Testament. In lieu of a God who walked in the Garden with Adam, Clement of Alexandria was describing a God "not then in space, but above space and time and name and conception."[12] In the Western Church the trend was more pronounced. "Neoplatonic thought," a blend of Greek philosophy and Eastern mysticism, "had affirmed the inaccessibility of God to the human mind, [and] viewed this inaccessibility as the result of the fallen character and of the soul."[13] Philosophy's influence soon overwhelmed the anthropomorphism of Genesis. The North African Tertullian agreed that God was invisible, incomprehensible, and inconceivable.[14] The problem that emerged in the wake of such a God was now considerable: "On the one hand, God must be utterly transcendent, unchanging, incorporeal, invisible, beyond the grasp and description of . . . intellect. . . . But, as God is also thought of as the provident, benign creator and ruler of all that is good, the question arose: how is God to reveal and achieve his benevolent, saving purposes when his transcendence makes it impossible for him to communicate with anything beyond himself?"[15]

A theologian of the Eastern Christian tradition, by contrast, writes that "the basic and original phenomenon of [Christian]

THE GOSPEL BEFORE THE RESTORATION

religious life is the meeting and mutual interaction between God and man, the movement of God towards man and man towards God."[16] This presupposes that *"God and man are related"* (our emphasis).[17] The familial relationship between God and man is soon lost, however, and in the Catholic West in particular, the conception of man as a mere creature became parlayed into a vast ontological gulf. In order to bridge this gap that was increasingly emphasized, Christ's function as mediator became paramount, in the sense of a God made flesh with whom finite creatures could identify. This role of Christ served to heighten the sense of distance between the invisible Father and his earthly creations. Even for early Church Fathers like Irenaeus, steeped in Greek philosophical influences, "there is absolutely no continuity between God and creation. . . . God and our world do not belong to the same continuum: there is nothing linking our world to its creator. Creation does not share in the same substance as God."[18] An emphasis on God's inaccessibility and total transcendence meant an increasing distance in what had been a relationship of intimacy and coeternal origins. Hence, the same Irenaeus preached that "the Father of all is at a vast distance from those affections and passions [sufferings] which operate among men."[19]

Other arguments were at work as well. Some early Christians, jealous for God's honor and glory, believed that diminishing the infinite distance between God the Father and the human would be a threat to God's majesty. Irenaeus argued that the Father guarded his invisibility "lest man should at any time become a despiser of God."[20] In his drive to emphasize infinite distance between God and man, Tertullian felt it necessary to jettison preexistence, which attributed to mankind "so large an amount of divine quality as to put it on a par with God."[21]

The trend of emphasizing radical distance and discontinuity between God and his children would accelerate in the centuries ahead, culminating in the Reformation concept of sovereignty. As John Sanders writes, the most appropriate analogy for the God-man relationship is that of a "king enacting a covenant with his vassal."²² This is a remarkable transition from the loving, vulnerable God of Christ, Paul, and the first Christians to the sovereign deity of the Reformation creeds. Origen had asked rhetorically, "Must [the Father] not then, in some sense, be exposed to suffering? So you must realize that in his dealing with men he suffers human passions. 'For the Lord thy God bare thy ways, even as a man bears his own son . . . ' Thus God bears our ways, just as the son of God bears our 'passions.' The Father himself is not impassible. If he is besought he shows pity and compassion; he feels . . . the passion of love . . . and for us men he endures the passions of mankind."²³

The sovereign God, by contrast, to harmonize with the ideals of the prevailing Greek philosophies of the era and to emphasize God's dissimilarity from humans, was stripped of passion and vulnerability. One scholar writes, "The idea that God cannot suffer, [was] accepted virtually as axiomatic in Christian theology from the early Greek Fathers until the nineteenth century."²⁴ This basic position was historically so uncontroversial, notes another scholar, that no challenge to the doctrine emerged between its defense in the third century and assorted critiques of the position in the late nineteenth century.²⁵ With the Protestant Reformation, the position was canonized in both the Thirty-Nine Articles of the Church of England and the subsequent Westminster Confession. The very first sentence of chapter 2 of the latter still reads as follows: "There is but one living and true God, everlasting without body, parts, or passions."²⁶ This Confession of Faith, approved by the English Parliament in 1648, established the basis of Reformed theology embraced by the Puritans and the Presbyterians. This document, which served as the basis of Baptist and Congregationalist theology as well, confirmed the impassibility of God. The result caused twentieth-century theologian Nikolai Berdyaev to lament that "the God whom official theology tends to construct has no profound relationship with men; he is turned to stone and man is humiliated."²⁷

As God becomes ever more inaccessible, unapproachable, invisible, and incomprehensible, then Christ assumes those characteristics of which God has been shorn: Jesus is the incarnate, approachable, entreatable God. In Trinitarian thought, it is Jesus to whom we relate, with whom we identify, and whom we approach as our intercessor. A proximate, approachable Christ is a wonderful thing, but not at the cost of losing the Father of absolute love. Jesus told his apostles that "he that hath seen me hath seen the Father,"[28] but theologians insisted on moving them poles apart, dismissing Christ's own words in the process. As a result, Augustine writes that the apostle Philip should not "assume that God is to be thought of in the same way as he saw the Lord Jesus Christ." Ambrose, the Bishop of Milan, writes that "I know of only one image, that is, the image of the unseen God." The French bishop Hilary of Poitiers agrees that "a corporeal Christ will not be the likeness of the invisible God, nor will a finite limitation represent that which is infinite," and so forth.[29]

Some few, like Theodore of Mopsuestia, took the Savior at his word: "There is no difference. . . . There is a perfect similarity between us two. . . . If you had known me, you would have known him too."[30] However, with the creedal formulations that stress incomprehensibility, and with the development of an atonement theology that emphasized a suffering Christ satisfying a God of uncompromising justice, the rift only grew. Christ embodies mercy where God is perfect justice; Jesus is all gentleness where the Father is all wrath. Rather than collaborators in the great plan of human happiness, Jesus is cast as our shield and protector against the inflexible demands of a sovereign God. In the most influential Christian poem of the English language, John Milton rendered the fraught relationship that threatens heavenly vengeance: "Th' Almighty Father from above, From the pure Empyrean where he sits/ High throned above all heights," foresees the coming Adamic drama, and rages against the race: "For man will hearken to [Satan's] glozing lies,/ And easily transgress the sole command, . . . So will he fall/ He and his faithless progeny: whose fault?/ Whose but his own? Ingrate, he had of me/ All he could have."[31]

The paternal tenderness rooted in premortal councils, where we were invited as coparticipants into a covenantal relationship that actively engages both parties, has largely disappeared. That father figure has been transformed into the Sovereign, in whose "supreme will resides the power which acts on the wills of all created spirits, helping the good, judging the evil, controlling all, granting power to some, not granting it to others . . . to whom all wills are subject."[32] Observes one historian of theology, Roger Olson, "Christian theology before Augustine tended to assume a view of the God-world relationship called synergism—the idea and belief that God's agency and human agency cooperate in some way to produce . . . salvation. . . . Pre-Augustinian theologians all assumed that God allows humans some degree of freedom to make . . . decisions." For Augustine, by contrast, "God's agency is all-determining in both universal history and individual salvation."[33] Augustine's biographer writes that God has been turned into "the imperial ruler of the universe, and what cannot be sacrificed at any price is the absolute *power* of that God. This is the guiding thread of Augustine's thought, that which gives shape to those doctrines most associated with his name."[34] And no figure between Paul and the Reformation was more influential on the development of Christian ideas than Augustine.

A thousand years after foundations were laid for a less kind and gentle God, Erasmus pleaded that "no one should despair of pardon from a God by nature most merciful;" Martin Luther fumed in response that Erasmus was "without Christ, without the spirit,"[35] because God "foresees, purposes, and does all things according to his immutable, eternal and infallible will."[36] The sovereign God of John Calvin, likewise, "foresees the things which are to happen . . . he has decreed that they are so to happen . . . it is clear that all events[, good and evil alike,] take place by his sovereign appointment."[37]

These beliefs in a God who does not just foresee or permit, but decrees and enacts his will through the world of nature, human history, and individual souls alike, were codified in the foundational creeds coming out of the Reformation, such as the Westminster Confession. Therein we read that "He is the alone fountain of all being, of whom, through whom, and to whom, are all things; and hath most sovereign dominion over them, to do by them, for them, or upon them, whatsoever himself pleaseth."[38] One can understand, reading these lines, why God would have condemned such creeds to the boy prophet Joseph. For they declare our Heavenly Father to be arbitrary, fickle, as content to damn as to save, all-controlling and manipulative. He foreordains to damnation, without reason or recourse. (And it is not because he foresees some will sin; the creed expressly states his decrees are *"without any foresight of faith"* or of wickedness.) Furthermore, these particular creeds emphasize his total independence from human concerns, human suffering, human conceptions of fairness, or human yearning to understand him. His counsels are "unsearchable," and his concern is only with "his own will." The accompanying catechism refers to his "fervent zeal for his own worship" and "his revengeful indignation" of incorrect forms of worship.[39] As for his pity or compassion or grief felt on our behalf, "these things are no more than . . . certain figures of speech, with which even schoolboys are acquainted."[40]

We do not doubt the sincere zeal of such Reformers. They were distressed by clerical abuses such as the sale of indulgences and the veneration of relics, unscriptural innovations such as devotion to the saints and the Virgin Mary, and what they saw as more reliance on sacraments than on piety. Nevertheless, the consequences of their theological innovations were fatal for Christian conceptions of the God known to Enoch, who confirmed man's agency in the Garden, mourned with and over his children, and was mighty enough to save them all.[41] A popular eighteenth-century school *Collection of English Prose and Verse* captured the religious terrors that had become increasingly normalized. One writer in the anthology agonized over "the vast uncertainty I am struggling with . . . the force and vivacity of my apprehensions; every doubt wears the face of horror, and would perfectly overwhelm me, but for some faint gleams of hope, which dart across the tremendous gloom. What tongue can utter the anguish of a soul suspended between the extremes of infinite joy or eternal misery. . . . I tremble and shudder."[42]

It is little wonder that, raised in such an environment, the young Joseph sought escape from such terrors. "Therefore I cried unto the Lord for mercy for there was none else to whom I could go," he wrote.[43] Without the prompt from James, that God would not "upbraid" such a request,[44] it is doubtful the young man would have found the courage to approach such a fearsome God.

CHAPTER 3

THE FALL

FROM EDUCATIVE TO CATASTROPHIC

He pronounced no curse against Adam personally, but against the ground. . . . The curse in all its fulness fell upon the serpent.

—IRENAEUS[1]

The original Christian story had been one that began with hope, with promise, with joyful anticipation: the human saga as an auspicious epic of ascent from primeval intelligence through mortal embodiment toward abundant life with God. In this original telling, rather than a story that is primarily about recuperation, repair, and rehabilitation, we begin "whole," if unrefined, "from the foundation of the world."[2] Philo of Alexandria, a Jewish contemporary of Jesus, taught that "after having for habitat and country the most pure substance of heaven," we transition into mortality. Reading the account in Genesis, he finds in the coats of *skin* with which God clothed Adam and Eve clear reference to the incarnation of their preexistent souls.[3]

The New Testament itself does not speak of Adam's fall as a sinful tragedy, but as the introduction of death into the world. ("In Adam all die," and "by one man . . . death passed upon all men.")[4]

THE FALL

One of the earliest influential voices in Christian theology was Irenaeus. Some lapses aside, the words of Irenaeus should have particular weight with Christians particularly since he was a disciple of Polycarp, who, according to tradition, was personally taught by John the Revelator.[5] The most accurate account of the Fall we find in early Christianity is, not surprisingly, that of Irenaeus. Irenaeus sees Adam's quick contrition as showing "confusion" rather than rebellion in his action. In a reading with an astoundingly familiar ring, Irenaeus explains the expulsion from the Garden as an act of mercy rather than punishment and exile:

> Wherefore also he drove him out of Paradise, and removed him far from the tree of life, not because he envied him the tree of life, as some venture to assert, but because he pitied him, [and did not desire] that he should continue a sinner for ever, nor that the sin which surrounded him should be immortal, and evil interminable and irremediable. But he set a bound to his [state of] sin, by interposing death, and thus causing sin to cease . . . so that man, ceasing at length to live to sin, and dying to it, might begin to live in God.[6]

Not only does Irenaeus see God's response as merciful rather than punitive, he interprets the transgression itself as necessary rather than catastrophic:

> Man has received the knowledge of good and evil. It is good to obey God, and to believe on him, and to keep His commandment . . . as not to obey God is evil. . . . Wherefore he has also had a two-fold experience, possessing knowledge of both kinds, that with discipline he may make choice of the better things. But how, if he had had no knowledge of the contrary, could he have had instruction in that which is good? . . . How, then, shall he be a God, who has not as yet been made a man?[7]

Origen also agreed that the Fall was necessary and educative, not tragic and misguided: "You (the soul) could not have reached the palm-groves unless you had experienced the harsh trials; you could not have reached the gentle springs without first having to overcome sadness and difficulties. . . . The education of the soul is an age-long spiritual adventure, beginning in this life and continuing after death."[8]

Responding to those who wondered why Adam had not been created more immune to sin, Irenaeus said that God organized all things from the beginning for "the bringing of man to perfection, for his edification, . . . that man might finally be brought to maturity at some future time."[9] One theologian calls "the notion that Adam was not created perfect, but rather . . . intended to come to be in the likeness of God at the end of a process of development" one of the "most characteristic" teachings of Irenaeus.[10] That "Adam and Eve were still children when they sinned was commonly accepted," not just by Irenaeus, but by others of the early Church Fathers—especially in the East.[11] In fact, the Eastern Church succeeded for some time in keeping alive an understanding of mortality as a step forward, not backward.

Adam was not a perfect being who fell; on the contrary, wrote Theophilus of Antioch, "Adam was created for development." At the time of their transgression, he and Eve were "infants" in maturity.[12] Robert Payne writes that "again and again in the writings of the Eastern Church Fathers there appears this singular devotion to the dignity of man. . . . In the West this devotion to the dignity of man is only occasional; in the East it is perpetual." As illustration, he quotes Gregory of Nyssa as writing that even after the Fall, "man's soul is a mirror in which he can see God. . . . You have only to return to the purity of the image established in you in the beginning. . . . There you will find purity, holiness, simplicity, all those gentle radiances of the divine nature."[13]

That divine nature attached to the physical body as well. A

THE FALL

thousand years later, with Luther soon to thunder forth about the human body, "what is more filthy?,"[14] the Eastern Church figure Gregory Palamas writes that "by the honor of the body created in the likeness of God, man is higher than the angels."[15]

These teachings were largely true to the gospel taught by Christ, his apostles, and many of those taught by the apostles or one generation removed from them, including Ignatius, Polycarp, and Irenaeus. Both Job ("in my flesh shall I see God") and Jesus explicitly affirmed bodily, physical resurrection ("a spirit hath not flesh and bones, as ye see me have").[16] Humankind's restoration to a physical tabernacle can only be taken therefore as divine affirmation of the body's eternal value. Tertullian celebrates the body with an exuberance seldom known in subsequent Christian traditions: "so intimate is the union, that it . . . [is] uncertain whether the flesh bears about the soul, or the soul the flesh." Consequently, whatever good the spirit accomplishes or perceives, it does so in partnership with a physical body: "For what enjoyment of nature is there, . . . what relish of the elements, which is not imparted to the soul by means of the body? Is it not by its means that the soul is supported by the entire apparatus of the senses—the sight, the hearing, the taste, the smell, the touch? Is it not by its means that it has a sprinkling of the divine power[?]"[17] In this view, "the flesh, which is accounted the minister and servant of the soul, turns out to be also its associate and co-heir."[18] His contemporary Clement of Alexandria agreed: the soul will only attain "its desired end" through the body, its "consort and ally."[19]

As Joseph found affirmed in the book of Moses, the Fall was enabling, not damning. Needing to pass through mortality as a stage in their eternal progress, all premortal spirits "were born into the world *by* the fall."[20] By the fourth century, Western Christianity had adopted a radically different reading of events. Irenaeus clearly believed and taught that "Human-kind needed to grow accustomed to bearing divinity through trial and gradual maturation"; Adam's action was "like the first fall of a baby just learning to walk."[21] Augustine, on the other hand, saw the Fall as regression and original sin as a disaster repaired only partially by Christ. With preexistence fading from Church teachings, Adam and fellow humans are not spirits sent here to undergo the crucible of mortal experience; they are flawless creatures whose fall was inexcusable. Human nature becomes deformed, and guilt and sensual appetite are the human inheritance. Unlike Olson, who believed earliest doctrines were less rather than more reliable, Anthony Zimmerman (more reasonably) holds the earliest to be more authoritative: "Irenaeus heard from Polycarp what the Apostles had taught. Augustine lived several centuries later. Very likely, then, there is no Apostolic Tradition which would affirm" Augustine's views, even though they soon overwhelm Irenaeus's more positive outlook.[22]

Even so, generous perspectives that see the Fall in a magnanimous light will emerge from time to time, as with the great fourteenth-century mystic Julian of Norwich. She described a vision in which she saw a preexistent Adam, whom she understood represented "all men and their falling."

> [God] sends him to a certain place to do his will. Not only does the servant go, but he dashes off and runs at great speed, loving to do his lord's will. [But] soon he falls into a [ditch] and is greatly injured; and then he groans and moans and tosses about and writhes, but he cannot rise or help himself in any way.

After his fall, Julian recorded that she attended carefully to the vision to know "if I could detect any fault in him, or if the lord would impute to him any kind of blame; and truly none was seen, for the only cause of his falling was his good will and great desire." In fact, the Lord explained to her that, since the servant undertook his task out of love and "good will," "is it not reasonable that I should reward him for his fright and his fear, his hurt and his injuries and all his woe," making him "highly and blessedly rewarded forever, above what he would have been if he had not fallen," culminating in "surpassing honour and endless bliss?"[23]

In other words, Julian understood that Adam and Eve—representing humanity—deserved neither censure nor punishment but a compensation even richer than the goodly state and condition they risked in going forth. Inspired others joined Julian in rejecting mortality as a cursed consequence of transgression, including a number of seventeenth-century poets, such as Thomas Traherne.

> *How like an angel came I down!*
> *How bright are all things here!*
> *When first among His works I did appear*
> *Oh, how their glory me did crown!*
> *The world resembled His eternity,*
> *In which my soul did walk;*
> *And everything that I did see*
> *Did with me talk.*[24]

In the twentieth century, Nikolai Berdyaev, a theologian and philosopher of the Eastern Orthodox tradition, wrote that "The fall of the first Adam was a necessary cosmic moment in the revelation of the new Adam. This was the way to a higher completeness."[25] We hear again such clear words of Adam and Eve's greatness in Elder John Widtsoe's teaching that "in life all must choose at times. Sometimes, two possibilities are good; neither is evil. Usually, however, one is of greater import than the other. When in doubt, each must choose that which concerns the good of others—the greater law—rather than which chiefly benefits ourselves—the lesser law. The greater must be chosen. . . . That was the choice made in Eden."[26]

However, prophets like Julian, Traherne, and Berdyaev were rare.[27] In place of this joy-filled recognition of childhood innocence and of mortality as a precious boon, Western Christian leaders and theologians emphasized doctrines of Edenic failure on a cosmic scale, Eve (and all women) as inherently weak and inferior, and humanity itself as the damaged detritus of a plan gone tragically wrong. Such beliefs were creedally formulated and rigorously enforced upon a Christian populace throughout the Middle Ages and into the age of Protestant Reformation. It would be impossible to exaggerate the damage done by the view of life as the consequence of moral failure rather than triumph, of human nature as depraved and evil rather than good but encumbered, and of Christ himself primarily as repairman of a cosmic catastrophe and shield against God's wrath, rather than the co-architect of an original plan of induction into the society of heaven.

CHAPTER 4

AGENCY

FROM FREE TO PREDETERMINED

Man is possessed of free will from the beginning, and God is possessed of free will, in whose likeness man was created.
—IRENAEUS[1]

God having placed good and evil in our power, has given us full freedom of choice.
—JOHN CHRYSOSTOM[2]

Little doubt existed in the early Church that humans were possessed of a free will; Christ had told his disciples that the truth made them free,[3] and that is why few doctrinal positions find such early unanimity. A contemporary of Irenaeus in the Eastern Church wrote in the second century that "[God] willed to save man by persuasion, not by compulsion, for compulsion is not God's way of working." As one commentator observes, "This pithy statement was evidently a common Christian saying in the second century since it is echoed nearly verbatim in several other documents from this era."[4]

The landscape changes dramatically with the rise of Pelagius, a monk probably born in Britain in the fourth century. A great believer in free will, his hostility to original sin and to the proponents of predestination led him to emphasize self-determination. As Augustine read him, "These new Pelagian heretics . . . claim that the choice of the will is so free that they leave no room for God's grace, which they claim is given in accordance with our merits."[5] It is possible if not probable that Augustine was exaggerating Pelagius's position; with no surviving manuscripts of the latter, we have only Augustine's word for what Pelagius was teaching. In any case, Augustine, who had labored to defend the freedom of the will, now felt it was necessary to abandon that principle and replace it entirely with grace. In his *Retractions*, written at the close of his life, he apologizes for his earlier stalwart defense of free will. "I, indeed, labored in defense of the free choice of the human will; but," he says tellingly (and "with a shudder," writes Robert O'Connell), "the grace of God conquered."[6] The Eastern tradition resisted this abandonment of free will: "Only this free, personal mind can commit sin and incur the concomitant 'guilt.' . . . There would be no place, then, in such an anthropology for the concept of inherited guilt, or for 'the sin of nature.' Sin is always a personal act, never an act of nature [because man's nature is Godward]." One Eastern Patriarch, Photios, went so far as to state that the Western doctrine of the "sin of nature" is heretical.[7]

Catholic tradition continued to have its proponents of both positions, but the Reformers of the sixteenth century and beyond revived Augustine's arguments forcefully. In fact, in founding the Reformed Church (or Calvinist tradition), Calvin would claim a millennium later that of all the Church Fathers, only Augustine understood that free will was a myth.[8] "There is no free will in man to resist" the salvation or the damnation God has predestined for us.[9] Luther, also, insists that free will "can be applicable to none but [God]." We, by contrast, "do all things from necessity, not from 'Free-will,'" and God "makes us necessarily damnable."[10] When he engages the Catholic moderate Erasmus in debate, Luther (or Dr. Hyperbolicus, as Erasmus affectionately calls him) at one point claims to have proven that, "'Free-Will' is thrown prostrate, and utterly dashed to pieces."[11] Man's salvation "is utterly

AGENCY

beyond his own powers, counsel, endeavors, will, and works, and absolutely depends on the will, counsel, [and] pleasure ... of God only."[12]

It is important to clarify that Calvin did not mean that in his sovereignty, God accords some freedom of action to men and so passively *permits or allows* all things, but that he actively *wills and ordains* all things, from Adam's fall to the Holocaust.[13] "God not only foresaw the fall of the first man, and in him the ruin of his posterity; but also at his own pleasure arranged it." Why did he so ordain it? "Because he saw that his own glory would thereby be displayed."[14] Calvin agrees with Luther that to claim that "in accordance with free-will, [man] was to be the architect of his own fortune" is a "frigid fiction" that denies "the omnipotence of God, by which ... he rules over all." He adds, "The decree, I admit, is dreadful."[15]

The major Protestant creed soon to emerge declared that "by the decree of God, for the manifestation of his glory, some men and angels are predestinated unto everlasting life, and others foreordained to everlasting death." Some few he will save, but for "the rest of mankind, God ... according to the unsearchable counsel of his own will, ... extendeth or withholdeth mercy as he pleaseth, for the glory of his sovereign power over his creatures, to pass by, and to ordain them to dishonor and wrath ... to the praise of his glorious justice."[16] Human agency began to make a comeback in the years prior to the Restoration, with the advent of a religious strain known as Arminianism, which tempered the Reformation doctrine of irresistible grace and of limited election by according more place to the will.

Unfortunately, Latter-day Saints continue to bear the legacy of the earlier fatalism in a vocabulary still too prone to ascribe the contingencies and vicissitudes of mortal probation to a foreordained destiny. As Joseph reminded his followers, "I believe that God foreknew everything, but did not foreordain everything."[17] Exaltation is within the reach of all, even if the journey toward that divine end is fraught with suffering. If we had insurance against a painful journey, one-third of the heavenly hosts would not have abandoned the enterprise. The risks are real. Or, in the language of the Book of Mormon, we cannot assume that our afflictions come from God, but we can know that "God . . . shall consecrate [our] afflictions for [our] gain," as Lehi promises his son Jacob.[18] We enter into a world, the Preacher of Ecclesiastes recognizes with sadness, of painful uncertainties and vulnerabilities to impersonal laws of nature and the agency of others. "I returned, and saw under the sun, that the race is not to the swift, nor the battle to the strong, neither yet bread to the wise, nor yet riches to men of understanding, nor yet favour to men of skill; but time and chance happeneth to them all."[19]

Neither should Latter-day Saints believe that "whatsoever comes to pass" is ordained of God, or that God is "the source of all that is."[20] Our Heavenly Parents do not arbitrarily decree the nature of good and evil, of joy and sorrow. They are divine beings because they embody a nature that is fully consistent with the nature of happiness. These divine beings, themselves supremely perfect, holy, and joyful, wished us to experience mortality in order to attain that same expansive life. They provide that experience not by arbitrarily inventing rules and requirements, but by articulating for us the contours of a moral universe that is coeternal with them. And because they have chosen to honor and preserve our agency, a great many things happen that they have not ordained, and that are entirely inconsistent with their will. From the cross words I spoke this morning to the drunk driving accident last night, from my father's cancer to the Holocaust, from rain on a wedding day to catastrophic earthquakes, ills and tragedies occur as a consequence of our choices, the choices of others, and the natural laws of our universe. As philosopher Paul Ricoeur wrote, in words that ring true for those who still carry intimations of costly premortal covenants: "This God delivers me up to the dangers of a life worthy of being called human."[21] God's omnipotence lies in what we have quoted elsewhere as the divine power "to alchemize suffering, tragedy, and loss, into wisdom, understanding, and even joy."[22] "Other things, other blessings, other glories," C. S. Lewis writes. "God can make use of all that happens."[23]

CHAPTER 5

Sin

FROM PAIN AND SUFFERING TO INHERENT DEPRAVITY

There is a portion of good in the soul, of that original, divine, and genuine good, which is its proper nature. For that which is derived from God is rather obscured than extinguished.
—TERTULLIAN[1]

*Man is in part divine,
A troubled stream from a pure source.*
—GEORGE GORDON, LORD BYRON[2]

Only one consequence of partaking of the forbidden fruit in the Garden of Eden was indicated by God to Adam—and it was death. It was this death that to early Church Fathers was the great tragedy in need of remedy. And that remedy was accomplished in Christ's resurrection. This was and remains the Eastern Christian mantra, that "as in Adam all die, even so in Christ shall all be made alive."[3] (Such is a Book of Mormon emphasis as well: "O how great the goodness of our God, who prepareth a way for our escape from the grasp of this awful monster; yea, that monster, death and hell, which I call the death of the body, and also the death of the spirit. And because of the way of deliverance of our God, the Holy One of Israel, this death, of which I have spoken, which is the temporal, shall deliver up its dead; which death is the grave."4) The universal inheritance of Adam's choice is death, not sin. Immersion in the world is not punishment, it is education.

As Irenaeus explained, God

> expresses both the generosity of his giving, and our weakness, and the fact that we are possessed of free will. For because of his kindness he bestowed his gift upon us, and made men free, as he is free. Because of his foresight he knew men's weakness and the results of that weakness; but because of his love and his goodness he will overcome [the weakness] of . . . man. It was necessary that [the weakness of man's] nature should first be shown and afterwards be overcome, and mortality be swallowed up by immortality, corruptibility by incorruptibility [death by resurrection] and man become formed to the image and likeness of God, having received the knowledge of good and evil [joy and suffering].[5]

A consensus in the Eastern tradition holds that "the inheritance of the Fall [is] an inheritance . . . of mortality rather than sinfulness, sinfulness being merely a consequence of mortality."[6] The possibility of sin is the necessary side effect of agency in a mortal world; it is "behovely," or necessary, in Julian of Norwich's words, since only by it do we learn that sin bears bitter and painful fruit, and thereby we are enabled to actively choose and embrace the good. "I often wondered why," she wrote, "through the great prescient wisdom of God, the beginning of sin was not prevented. For then it seemed to me that all would have been well." She was answered with these words: "Sin is necessary, but all will be well, and all will be well, and every kind of thing will be well. In this naked word 'sin' our Lord brought generally to my mind all that which is not good, . . . nor can it be recognized except by the pain caused by it."[7]

Julian's appreciation of our exposure to pain and suffering and sin would occasionally find expression in other voices who sensed there was divine intention behind our mortal vulnerability. "Know that the impulse to wrong is never without use and benefit to the just person. . . . For the perfection of virtue comes of struggle," wrote Meister Eckhart.[8]

What we have described—with Julian and Eckhart as Western outliers—is typical of Eastern Christianity, "where Augustinian thought exercised practically no influence," and so "the significance of the sin of Adam and of its consequences for mankind were understood along quite different lines."[9] In the West, with Augustine, we find that sinfulness becomes the overarching legacy of Eve's and Adam's choice. The origins of a theory of original sin are complicated, but the doctrine took emphatic hold with Augustine's stamp. Thus, we find in him the first developed theory that unambiguously assigns actual guilt to, and justifies the infliction of eternal torments upon, Adam, Eve, and every descendant to the end of time. It is no exaggeration to say that Augustine's view of original sin was to "become the center of western Christian tradition."[10]

Following Augustine's lead, the first of the great Reformers, Luther, claimed that as a consequence of the Fall, "man . . . is with his whole nature and essence not merely a sinner but sin itself."[11] "Your works are examined and found to be all evil. . . . [There is] not an atom of virtue in you."[12] In the 1577 Lutheran *Formula of Concord*, original sin is defined not as a "slight corruption of nature, but . . . so deep a corruption that nothing sound or uncorrupted has survived in man's soul or body."[13] In fact, the same creed does "reject and condemn" the teaching that "man still has something good about him in spiritual matters—for example, the capacity . . . to initiate, to effect or to cooperate in something spiritual."[14]

At the same time as did the Lutheran Concord, the Church of England officially propounded the doctrine that the Fall entails "the fault" as well as "the corruption of the nature of every man," and for which "infection" we deserve God's wrath and damnation. Any attempts on our own to perform works of righteousness "have the nature of sin."[15] Sin "has complete possession of every soul," wrote Calvin.[16] The major Reformers, in other words, all denied that we could even "cooperate in something spiritual," leading to the claim that any saving righteousness can only be Christ's, and "imputed" to us "*as if* we were righteous" (emphasis in original).[17] As Calvin explained, "The only righteousness acknowledged in heaven being the perfect obedience to the Law," our salvation only occurs when the Father "clothes us in the innocence of Christ and accepts it as ours."[18] Or, in Luther's language, any righteousness associated with us is an extrinsic or "alien righteousness of Christ" bestowed on or imputed to believers. The sinner "can boast of and glory of whatever Christ possesses as though it were his or her own."[19] As with determinism and predestination, the legacy of original sin was already fading by Joseph Smith's day. However, because the Restoration was birthed in a culture thoroughly steeped in misconceptions regarding sin and salvation, we as Latter-day Saints often continue to bear that legacy of inherent depravity. An important goal of Joseph Smith's revelations was to free us from a burdensome heritage.

However, the belief that we are all sinners and unworthy of God's love is so seductive that we succumb, unwittingly, to the pervasive doctrines of Augustine. As we will explore in chapter 9, we have drunk so deeply at the Augustinian and Reformation fountains that we are often incapable of either perceiving or savoring the role Christ desires to play in our lives. The vocabulary of sin and guilt and damnation has too often overwhelmed the restored gospel's message of absolute love and powerfully grounded hopefulness. As Elder Neal A. Maxwell said, summarizing the almost universal misapprehension of overanxious Saints among us, we must learn to "distinguish more clearly between divine discontent and the devil's dissonance, between dissatisfaction with self and disdain for self. We need the first and must shun the second. . . . When conscience calls to us from the next ridge," he wrote, her purpose is to beckon not to scold.[20] Rather than continuing to frame our lives in terms of deficiency and inadequacy, we would benefit from the perspective of Irenaeus, who emphasized the forward-looking process in which we should be engaged: becoming "perfect[ed] . . . after the image and likeness of God."[21]

In the above sections, we have seen how in cradle rather than creedal Christianity, conceptions of our predicament were full of generosity and consolation. Heavenly Father established his covenant with us in the beginning, having in mind our eventual unification with him and Heavenly Mother. As children of divine parents, we were invited to be perfected and sanctified with the assistance of an atoning Savior, so that having acquired "the divine nature" we could live in holy sociality with other celestial beings. We were understood to be children of the Most High, and our Heavenly Parents' concern for us was and is intimate, familial, and compassionate. The Fall was anticipated as a deliberative step our first earthly parents would undertake to pave the way for our embodiment, that we might enter upon the educative, soul-stretching enterprise of life in this pain-strewn world. "And what is faith, love, virtue unassayed," asks Milton's Eve, referring to the safety and security of a sheltered Paradise.[22] Our freedom to choose, to "taste the bitter, that [we] may know to prize the good,"[23] was manifest in our original assent to the plan of happiness in divine assemblies. It was operative in the Garden and has been ever since.

We have also seen how those initially pure truths were largely displaced by an erroneous reconstruction of the plan of happiness as originally understood. Knowledge of premortal participation in those deliberative sessions was lost, and the Father acquired a Platonic immateriality, with distance, "otherness," and impassibility rather than intimacy, relation, and compassion his defining qualities—which morphed in turn into wrathful sovereignty. The Fall was taken to signal the abrupt rupture with an intended paradisiacal existence for humans, and the terrible consequences of sin—a corrupt and ineffectual will, guilt, and inherent depravity—were bequeathed upon us all.

Our purpose in tracing the above history is to illustrate that, inevitably and tragically, the replacement of an original understanding of the gospel by these frameworks and suppositions has left a lasting impact on how we conceive of Jesus Christ: his nature, his relationship to us, his mission in the world's history and in our personal lives and testimony. Since Mormonism emerges out of the Protestant world of the nineteenth century, it still bears the influences of that legacy. And our thesis is that these developments and their repercussions have left a lingering impact on our ability to fully appreciate what is revolutionary, distinctive, and beautiful about the Christ who was restored through Joseph Smith in this modern dispensation, and to whom we now turn.

PART 2

ALL THINGS MADE NEW

Do Latter-day Saints worship the same Christ as other Christians? The answer is not a simple one. As Joseph Smith said, "The fundamental principles of our religion are the testimony of the Apostles and Prophets, concerning Jesus Christ, that He died, was buried, and rose again the third day, and ascended into heaven; and all other things which pertain to our religion are only appendages to it."[1] So yes, of course we worship Jesus Christ as the Son of God, Redeemer of the world.

At the same time, the Restoration radically reshapes our understanding of his character and role as it emerged in preexistent councils, where he positioned himself to be our spiritual Father and to reunite us with our Heavenly Family, committing himself with unparalleled devotion to the project of our return. The Restoration reclaims Christ's Atonement as an act of healing. It reconstitutes us as whole beings by transmuting the damage and pain endured in life's educative crucible into sanctifying suffering that expands our capacity to receive and give love. Then Jesus invites us to share in his work of healing and saving.

The Restoration also reconstructs judgment and salvation: the first as a process of self-understanding and self-revelation that is merciful and formative, the second as an eternal process by which an infinitely devoted Healer will work tirelessly to draw us ever onward into eternal realms of belonging.

CHAPTER 6

THE SELFLESS CHRIST

He doeth not anything save it be for the benefit of the world.
—2 NEPHI 26:24

Regardless of the religious or moral premises with which we begin, most philosophers and legislators can agree upon a few basic principles. Foremost of these is the assertion that human beings have a right to self-determination. The Universal Declaration of Human Rights adopted by the world community of nations in 1948 is so emphatic on this point that it employs forms of the word *free* thirty times in its short manifesto.[1] We have a right to freedom from slavery, from forced marriage, from labor or sexual exploitation, and a hundred other abuses. We could put this another way: The highest right we have is to be treated as an "I" and not an "it," a subject and not an object, a person with our own desires, interests, and intentions rather than a means to another person's ends. In this view of things, anything that turns us into an "it," an object, a means or instrument or vehicle of another person's interests or intentions, would be evil.

We think this is a powerful moral insight. Virtually all human evils can be interpreted in the light of this basic premise. Human trafficking, pornography, theft, fraud, rape—or more subtle evils, such as flattery, high-pressure sales, emotional manipulation—these and a thousand other varieties of wrongdoing objectify and instrumentalize other human beings. What greater perversity could we imagine than to take a human being made in the likeness and image of God and reduce her or him to a mere object among objects, a rung on the ladder of our own self-interest, a stepping-stone on the path to our own self-aggrandizement, or a disposable diversion in our pursuit of a self-serving aim? Such, however, is the nature of most any human evil one could name.

In this light, the God of Western Christian understanding has been endowed with some rather disturbing characterizations over time. Christianity began, as Origen demonstrated, with the knowledge that "God does not desire to make himself known for his own sake, but because he wishes to bestow upon us the knowledge of himself for the sake of our salvation, in order that those who accept it may become virtuous, and be saved," and be converted into "friends of God."[2] Irenaeus similarly taught that "we were not made gods at our beginning, but first we were made men, then in the end, gods. God does this out of the purity of his goodness, that none may think him envious or ungenerous."[3] Regrettably, this vision of a selfless God was short-lived. Tertullian's version of God "brought forth from nothing this entire mass of our world, with all its array of elements, bodies, spirits, for the glory of his [own] majesty."[4] In the seventeenth century, the English Puritan Thomas Watson asked his congregation, "What is the chief end of man?" and replied, "Man's chief end is to glorify God."[5] According to the great American divine Jonathan Edwards, God "always acts for his own glory and honor."[6] The first lesson of the Baltimore Catholic catechism asked, "Why did God make you?" The answer: "God made me to know him, to love him, and to serve him."[7] This view of God continues into the twenty-first century. One of the most popular preachers of our era writes, "You were made for God's glory."[8] An evangelical author of more than forty books likewise writes that "God loves his own glory above all things."[9]

Some Latter-day Saints may not recognize how Mormon thought ruptures radically with such a long-standing Christian view

THE SELFLESS CHRIST

of our relationship to God and returns us to early Christian roots. Defying centuries of such conceptions of divine sovereignty and self-absorption, Joseph Smith's teachings soothe with the healing balm of simple, uncomplicated, refreshing goodness: "What was the design of the Almighty in making man, it was to exalt him to be as God, the scripture says ye are Gods and it cannot be broken."[10] Brigham Young elaborated, "We are created, we are born for the express purpose of growing up from . . . manhood, to become Gods like unto our Father in heaven. That is the truth about it, just as it is. The Lord has organized mankind for the express purpose of increasing in that intelligence and truth, which is with God, . . . and becoming Gods, even the sons [and daughters] of God."[11]

The Book of Mormon affirms more simply: "Men are, that they might have joy."[12] Plato was closer to the gospel on this point than the larger portion of Christian theologians: "He who framed this whole universe . . . was good, and one who is good can never become jealous of anything. And so, being free of jealousy, he wanted everything to become as much like himself as was possible."[13] Not for his glory or happiness, but for theirs. In the words of Jehovah himself, God's work and glory is to bring to pass *our* immortality and eternal life.[14] Just as our Heavenly Mother and Father desire our eternal joy ("that is their goal, their work, and their glory," said Elder Theodore M. Burton[15]), Christ made that his *only* endeavor, for he "doeth not *anything* save it be for the benefit of the world" (our emphasis).[16]

Marvelous is the knowledge that Christ the Lord has made our eternal welfare the central motive of his holy existence, rather than the other way around. The God and Christ whom Latter-day Saints worship are demonstrably different from other versions. Our Heavenly Parents created us for our glory, not for theirs, and Christ orients his entire divine activity around the grand project of bringing us to where he is. How can we not adore such a one? It can truly be said that never has a body of disciples been given greater reason to love and reverence their God and their Savior.

CHAPTER 7

THE ADOPTIVE CHRIST

*At the first organization in heaven we were all present
and saw the Savior chosen and appointed, and the
plan of salvation made and we sanctioned it.*

—JOSEPH SMITH[1]

To say we sanctioned the plan of salvation is to say we were co-participants in God's designs for the human family. This is an astounding assertion. The plan, in its full version, would be called the new and everlasting covenant. (The covenant was "new" in the sense that disobedience had introduced the temporary schoolmaster of the Mosaic law, to be in effect until the original full covenant was restored with Christ.)[2] It is a system of covenants designed to shepherd us through the process of adoption into the divine family. Christ, through his absolute love and holiness, became fully human. The firstborn in the spirit became the only begotten in the flesh, God the Son, in order that he could become our Good Shepherd, break the bands of death, and open the doors to the more abundant life: "the glory which thou gavest me I have given them, . . . I will that they also, whom thou hast given me, be with me where I am."[3] If sometimes it seems we are adopted by Christ, and sometimes as children of God, that is because adoption operates in both those two senses. As the First Presidency clarified in a doctrinal exposition, the title of Father "has reference to the relationship between [Christ] and those who accept His Gospel and thereby become heirs of eternal life." At the same time, "by obedience to the Gospel men may become sons of God, both as sons of Jesus Christ, and, through Him, as sons of His Father."[4]

The unparalleled insight this gives us into the nature of Christ is that it places him in the role of proactively seeking our benefit—from before the world's foundation. And it reveals him as seeking our eternal companionship in a heavenly family. Rather than a rescuer of a plan gone awry, Christ is revealed as truly the author of our salvation from the beginning. The beauty of this background is that it reshapes everything. Cardinal Walter Kasper, in representing the current position of the Catholic Church, noted the catastrophe that launched mankind's history: "The human being wanted to be like God."[5] And one widely read historian of Christianity, Roger Olson, defines salvation thus: "God's purpose and goal in redemption is to reverse the sin, corruption and death introduced into humanity by Adam."[6] In this view, salvation is recuperative, reparative, restorative. Surely Christ can and does fulfill those functions. But how different a conception of his grand designs is indicated by a now mostly obscured picture, one in which earlier Church Fathers expressed "belief in salvation as a sacramental process of *theosis*—'divinization' or 'deification.'"[7] This is no return to a primordial condition, but a transcendence and progression beyond any earthly origin. Sin and death are not the beginning of the human saga; divine parentage and a planned celestial destiny are. Christ's central purpose from the beginning was not to correct an Adamic misstep, but to draw us further into a world of joyful sociality. His voluntary mission was not to take us *back* to an original condition, but to move us *forward*—from primeval wholeness ("whole from the foundation of the world") to a more abundant existence ("added upon").[8]

Sin, pain, and wounding occur along the way—they are part of our education. To talk of salvation from this perspective, however, is to talk of a process of addition, not recuperation. That was Joseph's understanding from the beginning. As was taught in the School of the Prophets, "What situation must a person be in in order to be saved? . . . if we can find a saved being, we may ascertain without much difficulty what all others must be in order to be saved." Christ "is the prototype or standard of salvation; or, in other words, . . . a saved being, . . . a just and holy being."[9] Salvation, then, is not rescue from condemnation, or a return to Eden. Salvation is the culmination of our richer incorporation into the heavenly family of celestial beings, in a healed and sanctified condition. We enter into a heavenly "kin-dom," rather than kingdom.

The difference in perspective is evident in the two functions we associate with baptism. Latter-day Saints, like many Christians, consider baptism important "for the remission of sins."[10] That is not its sole function, however, and a shift in emphasis could redirect our attention to its more glorious purpose as the first ordinance in the new and everlasting covenant—or as what Nephi calls "the gate by which we . . . enter" a process culminating in eternal life.[11] Theodoret of Cyrus, an Eastern contemporary of Augustine, considered remission of sins "a side effect of baptism," its central purpose being "a promise of greater and more perfect gifts, . . . a participation in his resurrection."[12] Joseph understood baptism in the same way: "One should "subscribe [to] the articles of adoption," he said, in order to enter into the celestial family.[13] We have all become separated from the divine family by physical distance—our introduction into mortality—as well as by harmful choices. As a result, we require a cleansing, healing, spiritual rebirth through formal "'adoption' into the heavenly kingdom, and into sonship [and daughtership] with God." This is possible because, as B. H. Roberts explained, we are "by nature the [children] of God."[14]

In placing adoption at the very heart of LDS theology, Joseph was making temporary separation rather than sin the principle factor in our present condition, and proper relation rather than righteousness the remedy. This is why the words of the covenant associated with baptism emphasize the adoptive effects of the ordinance. In Enoch's magnificent ascension experience, he is told that God wishes for us to *choose* him as Father.[15] We pledge to enter Christ's family by taking his name upon us in a formal act of adoption.[16]

This is a cardinal aspect of baptism. Nephi clearly states that we are adopted, that is, we "take upon [ourselves] the name of Christ, by baptism."[17] Alma confirms that baptism is a deliberate, formal covenant of adoption ("as a witness before him that ye have entered into a covenant with him").[18] We are signifying our desire to become part of his family and be called by his name. In the early Latter-day Saint church, members formally repeated the terms of the covenant at water's edge (presumably from Mosiah 18).[19] Baptism initiates us into the family of God, with Christ as our spiritual father. The First Presidency affirmed this meaning in 1916, explaining that "Men [and women] may become children of Jesus Christ by being born anew."[20] We no longer articulate our desire to be adopted prior to immersion, but each week we reaffirm this desire to be adopted by Christ. We pledge to "take upon [us] the name of [the] Son."[21] There is a lovely echo here of how baptism was understood in the Church's first centuries in the East. Ignatius called the Lord's Supper "the medicine of immortality," the first ordinance in our eventual "divinization or deification."[22] In the primitive Church, converts were often baptized in large groups at Easter, since the significance of both was birth to a new life.[23]

Lest there be any doubt that baptism signifies our first formal compliance with the original everlasting covenant by which we are integrated into God's family, the Lord affirmed that fact by revelation. "This is a *new and an everlasting covenant*, even that which was *from the beginning*," he said regarding the ordinance of baptism.[24] In the earliest Christian Church, after being washed and anointed, the baptismal candidate was clothed in new garments.[25] It is worth noticing that Genesis has God clothing Adam and Eve—and instructing them in the gospel—*after* they have eaten the fruit, not before. This makes good sense in Mormon theology, for Latter-day Saints understand the action as a step forward in the covenantal relationship, whereby "[they have] become as one of us," in the scriptural account.[26] In dramatic contradistinction to the Christian thought of Joseph's day, the couple Adam's[27] transgression is the action that puts them in a place to continue their progress in the everlasting covenant that is not rendered void in them but fully operative. Hence, the "angel of the Lord appeared unto Adam,"[28] revealing further gospel precepts followed by their actual baptism.

As Elder Carlos E. Asay explained, "Prior to their expulsion from the Garden of Eden, [but *after* partaking of the forbidden fruit,] Adam and Eve were clad in sacred clothing. . . . They received this clothing in a context of instruction on the Atonement, sacrifice, repentance, and forgiveness. The temple garment given to Latter-day Saints is provided in a similar context."[29] This sacred clothing is an affirmation of the covenant's continuing efficacy, not its abrogation. Theodoret of Cyrus described the early Christian ritual that linked baptism and sacred clothing in a new garment as "a mantle of salvation, a tunic of gladness, a garment of light."[30]

Like baptism itself, the garment captures a movement of integration rather than remediation, of a planned sequence in the eternal covenant rather than an act of repair. It confirms a further stage in the unfolding of the eternal covenant relationship under conditions that were fully anticipated and divinely sanctioned, leading to the embodiment of the human family as the posterity of Adam and Eve ("the mother of all living"[31]). In Eve's remarkable view that reverses two thousand years of reading Genesis: "Were it not for our transgression we never should have had seed, and never should have known good and evil, and the joy of our redemption."[32] In Joseph's concise formulation, God "fore-ordained the fall of man."[33]

CHAPTER 8

THE ATONING CHRIST

*. . . that he may know according to the flesh how to
succor his people according to their infirmities.*
—ALMA 7:12

One epithet attached to Christ that can mislead in unfortunate ways is that of "mediator." Warring nations may employ mediators. Contending spouses may make use of mediators. And antagonistic strikers and management are often assigned them. Mediation carries the implication of hostile parties with opposing agendas, competing interests, or simmering antipathies. With the increased distancing and impersonalization of God in the immediate post-apostolic era, Christ's role as collaborator with the Divine Parents shifted to become mediator between two disparate realms and orders of beings. In the Christian West, with its emphasis on sin as rebellion against God's "rigid interdiction,"[1] Christ's role as mediator became that of our shield and defender against the wrath and vengeance of a sovereign God. The history of atonement theology is too long and complex to trace here. But we hope that from our review of a distinctive LDS theology of God's true nature, the divine rationale for a Fall, and the nature of sin and human responsibility, our apprehension of the Atonement might be shaped accordingly. It would be distinct from the many models of penal substitution common throughout Christian history: that God, embodying justice, demands a penalty for sin, and Christ redirects God's vengeance onto himself.

Elder B. H. Roberts, who delved into the Mormon theology of atonement perhaps more than any other LDS authority, suggested that we should not see "justice" as some abstract, cosmic universal, nor as the inflexible standard of a legalistic heavenly monarch. It is, rather, another name for what, from a human perspective, guarantees the integrity of human choice. Choice must be choice *of something*. In John Stuart Mill's classic treatment, human liberty requires the freedom "of doing as we like, *subject to such consequences as may follow*" (our emphasis).[2] If choice is to be more than an empty gesture of the will, more than a mere pantomime of decision making, any given choice should eventuate in the natural consequence of that choice. What kind of freedom would it be, or what the value of human agency, if choices bore no fruit? White noise and secondhand smoke continually complicate the degree of freedom and accountability behind human choice. Paul's analogy of seeing "through a glass, darkly"[3] suggests that, in many instances, the complete and full exercise of choice is compromised and misjudgments are inevitable.

Of course, if consequences followed immediately and directly from actions, agency would likewise be compromised. Who would sin a second time if pain were the swift and inevitable result? Who would act from pure motive if virtuous actions unfailingly reaped manifold, immediate joys? Thus, we often navigate our way through turbulent seas under dark skies. Or, as Pope John Paul II described our mortal journey: we all face "a long crossing in little boats."[4] However, even allowing for mitigating circumstances and uneven playing fields that afflict us all, moral agency clearly requires a stable framework within which our choices are rendered meaningful and purposeful. "The quality of regularity . . . is necessary to a sense of security," in Roberts's language.[5]

In other words, he clarifies that we might better consider that certain "consequences," rather than imposed penalties or rewards, follow our choices. Hence the validity, the efficacy, of our very agency, rather than some abstract justice, is what is at stake in the expectation that consequences indeed follow upon the exercise of human agency. This is why the Book of Mormon emphasizes the urgency of being "instructed sufficiently" in the workings of the universe, the laws that govern pain and happiness, the nature of choice and consequence, so that we may "free[ly] choose liberty and eternal life."[6]

In this schoolroom of mortality, with our knowledge still imperfect, our wills not yet purified, and our character not fully formed, we too often choose poorly. It was in precise anticipation of such weakness that our Savior was appointed, before earth's creation, to bear the burden of pain that follows in sin and error's wake. Christ assumes the full weight of the aftershocks of our actions in our place (he "suffered these things for all, that they might not suffer").[7] Since genuine moral agency must entail necessary consequences, Christ, according to the language of scripture, volunteers himself an offering to assume the painful consequences of our injurious choices. Appeasing some abstract justice, or propitiating a sovereign God, is *not* the point. The preservation in the universe of real opposites, and real stakes, in order to assure the efficacy of agency, *is*. Thus, guaranteeing "security" and "regularity" in the universe's workings, and emphasizing consequence rather than "satisfaction" or "penalty," are seismic shifts beyond the medieval categories of atonement theology, and represent a genuinely Mormon theology of atonement. One might call it a "choice and consequence" theology, one oriented around the preservation and validation of agency and education rather than around divine government or justice.

The alternative to this scenario would be a universe in which freedom is effectively nonexistent because choices do not matter, opposites collapse, and, as Lehi describes, "all things must needs be a compound in one,"[8] with no righteousness and consequently no happiness. The coexistence of opposites, in order to facilitate the ability of humans to choose for themselves between the bitter and the sweet, must be maintained inviolate for the proving of contraries. It is only through the experience of good (joy) and evil (suffering) that truth is made manifest and progress toward inculcating the divine attributes is enabled.[9] In the absence of that essential connection of choice to consequence, agency is nullified. This is what was at stake in Lucifer's counterproposal to the Father's plan. His way would have spared us immense suffering, but at the cost of our agency, its attendant educative effects, and thus the path toward the divine nature and the joy known only to those who have tasted the bitter.[10] Christ's intervention, in assuming the burden of human pain we bring upon ourselves and others, thus affirms the law of restoration, the cosmic order whereby human agency is guaranteed by the unfolding of consequences in accordance with law. God stands as a surety for our moral agency and our progression toward divinity.[11]

The assumption of the terrible burden of individual and collective human suffering and death empowered Christ to release mankind from both. The full extent of his sacrifice was accomplished by his voluntary experience of the most profound consequences of human misery and suffering. We cannot fathom a more-than-mortal fear that made the Creator himself hesitate to drain the cup to its dregs. Only a love borne out "even to the edge of doom" could have prevailed.[12] On the precipice of a critical moment of covenant making, "a horror of great darkness fell upon" Abraham.[13] At the Restoration's cusp, another prophet described how "thick darkness gathered around me, and it seemed to me for a time as if I were doomed to sudden destruction."[14] The stakes being infinitely greater in this case, the abyss into which Christ stared would have been infinitely more terrifying. This marked the beginning of Christ's final battle against Satan, the destroyer, which would indeed culminate in the death of the Son of God.

However, as Gregory of Nyssa wrote, in Christ's death lay the "seed of immortality."[15] As the book of Leviticus portended with sacred irony that Satan failed to comprehend: "For the life of the flesh is in the blood."¹⁶ The death of the Son of Man would eventuate in eternal life to those souls for whom he was now contending in the Garden of Gethsemane. Pictorial renditions of the deposition from the cross stamp the faces of the mourning family and disciples of Christ with Satan's triumph. However, Satan "knew not the mind of God," and, in seeking "to destroy the world," he in fact provided the space for Christ not only to save the world but to give mankind new life, "an inheritance incorruptible, and undefiled . . . reserved in heaven for you."[17]

Elder Jeffrey R. Holland suggested that Christ's abandonment by God on Calvary was the final stage of his cosmic ordeal, and described his "concluding descent into the paralyzing despair of divine withdrawal when He cries in *ultimate* loneliness, 'My God, my God, why hast *thou* forsaken me?'"[18] The suffering incurred by divine abandonment is beyond human comprehension. Christ's very real participation in human despair, loneliness, and the fear of being forsaken work in him a perfect understanding of the human condition. The absolute love here enacted is what "draws" all mankind to a reorientation of heart and mind and a consequent movement to a more complete self. The God with us (Immanuel) conquers death—the last enemy—thereby prying open the gates that had barred the way to our own resurrection from the dead. In both these ways, our alienation from God is overcome. We are physically brought back into his presence, and we are enabled to learn, from tasting the bitter fruit, to embrace the good and, with the sanctifying power of the Holy Spirit, prepare ourselves to be the children of God in very fact. It is principally in *that* sense, by fulfilling *those* functions, that Christ is our mediator.

As Irenaeus understood that mediation two thousand years ago, "The Word was made the *minister of the Father's grace* [love, kindness], for man's benefit. For man he wrought his redemptive work."[19] And it is precisely in this sense that we can understand the author of Hebrews calling Christ "the mediator of the new covenant," and

Joseph Smith's use of the same language, when he referred to "the mediator of the new covenant, who wrought out this perfect atonement."[20] Mediation, in this context, refers to Christ's serving as an instrument by which a desired purpose or harmony is achieved. And that is precisely what Christ does. He brings about our soul's healing, mending fractured relationships, resolving our temporary alienation from our Heavenly Parents, and effecting a more whole and holy selfhood. In this role, Christ is not protecting us from divine anger or judgment. On the contrary, Christ is collaborating with our Heavenly Parents for our homecoming.

Joseph F. Smith taught that "Jesus had not finished his work when his body was slain, neither did he finish it after his resurrection from the dead."[21] In the most sublime irony of all history, it was the emptiness of the Easter tomb—the words "he is *not* here"—that signaled the full and continuing presence of Christ in the world. Most Christians believe in a living Christ—though in what form or manner a post-resurrection, embodied Christ exists today in a Trinity without body, parts, or passions is not clear. (The Eastern Father Ignatius testified that after His death, Christ "was in the flesh, and I believe that He is still so.")[22] Joseph Smith's exultant claim that "he lives! For we saw him,"[23] is but one instance of a Christ newly and conspicuously engaged—again—in the ongoing stream of history and personal salvational experiences alike. One Restoration scripture in particular conveys with poignant and sacred intimacy the present, actual, "nowness" of Jesus' preoccupation with his spiritual brothers and sisters. "Hearken unto my voice," he pleads. "Listen to him who is the advocate with the Father, who is pleading your cause before him . . . that [you] may come unto me and have everlasting life."[24]

What, exactly, is meant in this verse? We are happy to know we have an advocate, but we would hope our Father is not in need of heart softening. That sounds too much like the sovereign God of Augustine, Calvin, and Milton, the absolute monarch before whom subjects quail. It may be that we misunderstand the term *advocate* in the way it is being used here: the expression appears once, and only once, in the King James Bible. In 1 John 2:1, in words echoed in the revelation to Joseph Smith, the apostle writes, "If any man sin, we have an *advocate* with the Father, Jesus Christ." The Greek term is *paraclete*, and that word appears five times in John's writings. The word first appears in John 14, as Jesus is spending his final evening with his apostles. In his tender regard for them, displacing his own concern for the terrors that await him, he says, "And I will pray the Father, and he shall give you another [paraclete]" to "abide with you for ever; . . . These things have I spoken unto you, being yet present with you. But the [paraclete], which is the Holy Ghost, . . . shall teach you all things, and bring all things to your remembrance, whatsoever I have said unto you."[25] In both the above instances, King James translators rendered *paraclete* as "comforter," not "advocate."

The paraclete, therefore, whom God will send, and of which the scriptures frequently testify, is the Holy Spirit, in the role of Comforter. This clarifies Joseph's use of the term *advocate* perfectly, because we have seen that scripture uses both *comforter* and *advocate* as the English equivalent of *paraclete*. Comfort, not judicial defense, is the purpose of a paraclete. Jesus promised a comforter, not a legal counsel, to those apostles who would soon bear the gospel to a hostile world, suffering trials, persecutions, and execution. Rather than a judicial advocate, they would need a helper, a sustainer, a teacher—someone to comfort them in times of distress and danger. And that is what the Lord promises them—the Holy Spirit as Comforter.

Also of significance, when Jesus tells his beloved friends he "will not leave [them] comfortless,"[26] the actual word he uses means "orphans" (ὀρφανός/orphanos). His disciples will not be cut off from the Heavenly Family; the process of spiritual adoption that commenced with their baptism will continue to unfold. They will be tended to perpetually with divine, parental love and care. As Elder Holland testified, "What would this world's inhabitants pay to know that

Heavenly Parents are reaching across . . . stream and mountains and deserts anxious to hold them close."[27]

Finally, if—as Christ says—it is the Father who is sending the paraclete, or comforter, then it hardly makes sense to see a paraclete's role as defending one *against* the Father. As a Greek scholar notes, in John's usage it is clear that the paraclete "is not the defender of the disciples before God but their counsel in relation to the world."[28] So when the Lord—following John's phrasing—assures the Prophet Joseph that we have an "advocate" with the Father, even Jesus Christ, he is repeating the promise given the apostles; we have in this case, too, a paraclete or advocate *alongside* the Father, *with* the Father. However, in this instance the advocate is the Son in *his* role as our comforter, our healer and spiritual helper. Once again we see that Christ as the atoning one—the mediator—is not our defender from God's justice, but the collaborator in and the minister of our Heavenly Parents' plan.[29]

Latter-day Saints are fortunate in that the temple gives them access to an experience of the Atonement's power that is even more sacred and impactful than the weekly sacrament. Joseph's greatest act of synthesis, wherein he drew Old Testament typology and New Testament teaching into harmony, was evident in the way he was inspired to depict temple architecture and design temple ritual so as to bring all things together in Christ. The key to his final effort may have been his reading of Hebrews and the light it shed on Abraham's unusual rite in Genesis 15. In that account, in token of the covenant he has entered into with God (the new and everlasting covenant), Abraham is commanded to sacrifice a heifer, a goat, and a ram (along with two birds). He then divides each large carcass into two halves. Subsequently, as Moses experienced before his theophany and Joseph before his, Abraham experiences "an horror of great darkness." And then the divine manifestation occurs: "a smoking furnace, and a burning lamp . . . passed between those pieces," following which the Lord personally affirms his covenant with Abraham.[30]

THE ATONING CHRIST

Explicating Old Testament sacrifices in light of the new covenant, the author of Hebrews invites the Christian to complete the pilgrim's journey by entering into the presence of God himself—"to enter into the holiest."[31] And the meaning of all prior sacrificial victims now becomes clear, as the author explains that entry into God's presence can only be "by the blood of Christ." Christians all know that the sacrificial animal is a type and foreshadowing of the Savior's death. But the writer of the letter to the Hebrews pushes the analogy further. We "enter into the holiest by the blood of Christ." We effectively pass *through* Christ's broken body, as the lamp of the Lord passed through the severed sacrificial creatures, and back into God's presence. The Atonement is the pain-drenched portal through which alone access is to be found. And in the author's final invocation of symbolism, he directs our minds to the image of the temple veil, which becomes the physical counterpart to the body of Christ, through which we pass into the holiest place. The writer of the letter says this explicitly: The "new and living way, which he hath consecrated for us" is "through the veil, that is to say, his flesh."[32]

In our temples, as in the Jewish temple, the veil represents the portal into the divine presence. The temple veil, the emblem of Christ's own flesh, was torn at the crucifixion, suggesting that only through the broken body of the atoning Savior was access into God's presence possible for all. This startling image, replicated in the temples of the Latter-day Saints, captures the quintessence of the temple's purpose. It signifies the eternal human saga by which men and women progressively constitute fuller and richer relationship to Divine Parents. The story tracks their pilgrimage from incarnate spirits, through adoption into Christ's family, assuming greater levels of commitment and higher standards of holiness, entering into binding covenants that reify and extend human and divine connectedness, until, cleansed and sanctified by the sacrificial offering of Christ's own flesh, they enter into the divine presence, part of an eternal sociality with those they love. The rituals of the temple are thus where the Church's most concentrated liturgical forms are found, and they crescendo with palpable crucifixion imagery at the veil, that symbolic, porous membrane joining heaven and earth. It is through the Atonement, through the severed flesh of Christ, typified in sacrifices that hark back to Adam himself, that all find full incorporation into the Heavenly Family, in accordance with the new and everlasting covenant that was propounded before the world was formed.

CHAPTER 9

THE HEALING CHRIST

Who is this that cometh from Edom, with dyed garments from Bozrah? this that is glorious in his apparel, travelling in the greatness of his strength? I that speak in righteousness, mighty to save.
—ISAIAH 63:1

And she shall bring forth a son, and thou shalt call his name JESUS: for he shall save his people from their sins.
—MATTHEW 1:21

For some of us, our enemies still compass us about with destruction, and the flames of hell continue to trouble our sleep. We may not fear persecutors and oppressors, or devils with pitchforks. However, we feel bruised if not besieged, wounded if not terrorized. Language that spoke to a vulnerable, beleaguered nation, or to terrified congregations imagining Dante's demons and the furious flames of a Jonathan Edwards, still haunts many of us today. The history of salvation theology writ large is the story of our desperate attempts to escape the terrors of eternal torment. The advent of the Protestant Reformation could be said to have been set in motion by such fear. "My situation was that, although an impeccable monk, I stood before God as a sinner troubled in conscience, and I had no assurance that my merit would assuage him," recalls Luther in explaining the genesis of his personal journey that launched a cataclysm.[1]

We believe that most people both inside and outside the Church "are trying to do right," as Brigham Young said. "I am in the midst of Saints, or at least of those who profess to be Saints; and if they are not Saints, I think they are trying to become so with all their might."[2] Yet, we are weighed down. Few of us may feel on the precipice of damnation, but we all feel wounded and weary. Is there a language that can speak more meaningfully—yet truthfully—to our predicament?

Translators have difficult choices to make. The term most frequently rendered in the King James Bible as *save* is the Greek word *sodzo*, as in the passage from Matthew in the epigraph to this chapter. And he who saves is the *soter*, based on that same word. But when Luke used the identical term *sodzo*, it was to describe Jesus' act of curing the blind man of his affliction (Luke 18). Mark used *sodzo* when Jesus made the girl whole from the plague (Mark 5). And Matthew employed the term *sodzo* when the hemorrhaging woman, touching the Lord's hem, was restored to health (Matthew 9). In all these and numerous other cases, the word often translated as *save* is more aptly rendered *heal*. Jesus healed the blind, healed the girl of the plague, and healed the woman with the issue of blood. In other words, rather than render the Messiah's title of *soter* as *Savior*, we could with equal linguistic justification call him Jesus Christ, Son of God, *Healer* of the World. One virtue of such a substitution is that healing signals the beginning of a glorious journey now unfolding, while saving implies its end. And we are all very much in eternity's morning. In Joseph's favorite biblical translation, the word for *Savior* is *das Heiland*. *Heil* is from the verb *heilen* and means "to heal." *Land* denotes a geographical location. *Das Heiland* could, therefore, be translated correctly as "place of healing." In other words, our place of healing *is* Christ. Julian of Norwich emphasized this even more emphatically when she wrote: "The blessed woundes of oure Saviour be opyn and enjoye to hele us."[3]

THE HEALING CHRIST

Anthony Zimmerman adds yet another dimension to the word *sodzo*. He notes that the Latin word *salvans* (our *soter* in Greek), which Irenaeus "uses to designate Christ's role, does not have the narrow meaning of a Savior who merely pays a ransom to rescue sinners. The word *Savior* means to Irenaeus, and to the Greek Fathers typically, the more inclusive role of Sanctifier. . . . [Christ] is more than a repairman who reconditions a damaged product. He is an architect who builds the structure originally according to God's primal plan, and then reconditions it even more magnificently after Adam's temporary crash."[4] For the saintly Gregory of Nazianzus, "the reconciliation of God and man began to take place at the moment of the incarnation itself." In the flesh Christ "united to himself a complete and entire human nature, thereby healing it and ennobling it. It is the mind, not the body, that leads us into sin. So it is the human mind that is most in need of being healed and restored."[5]

Augustine preached a human race lost and fallen. Calvin emphasized our depravity, and Luther our incapacity for any virtuous action. The tenacious hold of original sin and human depravity were beginning to fade by Joseph Smith's era. One prominent nineteenth-century theologian, Charles Hodge, would continue to insist that this doctrine "is part of the faith of the whole Christian world."[6] However, a modern theologian declares that the language of original sin has become "a cultural embarrassment," and many would agree.[7] We believe Gregory of Nazianzus' beautiful perspective was once again manifest on the cusp of the Church's Restoration. In June 1829, as Joseph Smith was finishing his translation of the gold plates, he pronounced in the scope of one single sentence a diagnosis of the human condition, the source of our universal brokenness, and the promise of our healing. "Neither will the Lord God suffer that the Gentiles shall forever remain in that state of *awful woundedness* which . . . they are in, because of the plain and most precious parts of the Gospel of the Lamb which hath been kept back."[8]

In subsequent editions, the wording was changed to "awful state of *blindness*," and in a speculative reconstruction, one scholar of a published version of the Book of Mormon argues for "state of awful *wickedness*."⁹ That progression is a stunning illustration of the kind of disturbing shift that we humans are prone to make. Joseph's initial rendering of the verse captures the first and great truth of the human condition. We are all wounded, we are all in need of healing, and the Lord has our recuperation very much in mind from the beginning. The scriptural emphasis originally is on the Lord's understanding of the circumstances that have combined to exacerbate our vulnerability and pain—in this case a scriptural record (the Bible) from which God's most compassionate and benevolent facets have been "kept back" due to the removal of the "plain and most precious parts" of the gospel. Thus bereft, the scriptures we inherited tragically misrepresent a divine nature that Jacob 5, with its mourning, ever-solicitous Gardener, and Moses 7, with Enoch's account of a weeping God the Father, restore. Our tendency—almost irresistibly urged upon us by our Protestant heritage—is to move from seeing ourselves as wounded to calling our condition blindness, and then removing mercy and aggravating circumstances from the equation altogether and dwelling on our supposed "wickedness." Elder Dale G. Renlund has urged a vocabulary more consistent with this early Book of Mormon language:

> As the Good Shepherd, Jesus Christ views disease in His sheep as a condition that needs treatment, care, and compassion. This shepherd, our Good Shepherd, finds joy in seeing His diseased sheep progress toward healing. The Savior foretold that He would "feed his flock like a shepherd, . . . bind up that which [is] broken, and . . . strengthen that which [is] sick." Though apostate Israel was depicted as being consumed with sinful "wounds, and bruises, and putrifying sores," the Savior encouraged, exhorted, and promised healing.¹⁰

It is true that some Book of Mormon passages reflect a dour appraisal of human character, especially the words of King Benjamin that "the natural man is an enemy to God, . . . and will be, forever and ever, unless he . . . putteth off the natural man."[11] The expression "natural man" is, of course, Pauline. As Paul employs the term (in 1 Corinthians 2:12–15), it has reference to an *acquired* worldliness; it is not a statement about human ontology, inherited nature, or innate attributes. In his triple parallelism, the apostle contrasts "the spirit of the *world*" with the spirit that is "of *God*"; what "*man's* wisdom teacheth" with what "the *Holy Ghost* teacheth"; and "the *natural* man" with him "that is *spiritual*." The "spirit of the *world*," "*man's* wisdom," and the "*natural* man," then, all refer to something we pick up as mortal baggage. They are not an attribute of our original nature.

As an entire school of scholarship now concedes, Paul has been misread on this point for centuries by multitudes of theologians and laity, and the toll has been terrible.[12] The mid-sixth-century Christian rejection of Origen's beautiful doctrines of human nature and potential, writes one religious historian, resulted in the supremacy "of a Christian theology whose central concerns were human sinfulness, not human potentiality; divine determination, not human freedom and responsibility. . . . Christianity was . . . poorer for their suppression."[13] This is precisely our point, that Joseph's divinely appointed task was to rescue Christianity from such a dismal preoccupation with sinfulness, total depravity, inherited guilt, and kindred "abominations."

The former Bishop of Stockholm and Dean of Harvard Divinity School, Krister Stendahl, urged a healthy corrective to the Christian preoccupation with sinfulness, describing it as a misreading of Paul:

> The point where Paul's experience intersects with his . . . understanding of the faith, furthermore, is not "sin" with its correlate "forgiveness." It is rather when Paul speaks about his *weakness* that we feel his deeply personal pain. Once more we find something surprisingly different from the Christian language that most of us take for granted: it seems that Paul never felt guilt in the face of this weakness—pain, yes, but not guilt. It is not in the drama of the saving of Paul the

sinner, but it is in the drama of Paul's coming to grips with what he calls his "weakness" that we find the most experiential level of Paul's theology.[14]

"Pain, . . . not guilt." As another theologian characterizes recent scholarship on Paul: "The primary question being answered in these Pauline texts is *not* Martin Luther's anguished 'How may I, a sinner, find a gracious God?'"[15] For N. T. Wright as well, "the story is less about sinful individuals being rescued from judgment for guilt . . . and more about God's fulfillment of his purposes for all creation through Israel."[16] Western Christianity's fixation on the "plagued conscience" is a development Stendahl traces to Augustine three centuries after Paul, and then to the Reformers over a thousand years later.[17]

In this regard, Brigham Young showed considerable prescience in reading Paul. His remarks on the natural man are one of the most important doctrinal pronouncements he ever made, and are worth quoting in full:

> It is fully proved in all the revelations that God has ever given to mankind that they naturally love and admire righteousness, justice and truth more than they do evil. It is, however, universally received by professors of religion as a Scriptural doctrine that man is naturally opposed to God. Paul says, in his Epistle to the Corinthians, "But the natural man receiveth not the things of God," but I say it is the unnatural "man that receiveth not the things of God." . . . The natural man is of God. We are the natural sons and daughters of our natural parents, and spiritually we are the natural children of the Father of light and natural heirs to his kingdom; and when we do an evil, we do it in opposition to the promptings of the Spirit of Truth that is within us. Man, the noblest work of God, was in his creation designed for an endless duration, for which the love of all good was incorporated in his nature. It was never designed that he should naturally do and love evil. When our first parents fell from

their paradisiacal state, they were brought in contact with influences and powers of evil that are unnatural and stand in opposition to an endless life. So far as mankind yield to these influences, they are so far removed from a natural to an unnatural state—from life to death.[18]

Joseph Smith's expansive, ennobling innovation was to see our Heavenly Parents' plan—from the beginning—as being about human elevation rather than remedy, advancement rather than repair, exaltation rather than reclamation. One religious historian describes the entire array of nineteenth-century "deists and freethinkers, universalists, Stone-Campbell 'Christians,' Adventists, Christian Scientists" as a fractious rebellion against the Augustinian heritage, but he notes that only the "Mormons . . . abandoned predestination's entire substructure in original sin."[19]

At the same time, it would be wrong to conclude from the above that the Fall does not represent for Mormons, as for other Christians, a radical alteration of the human predicament. Mormonism *does* accept the prevalence of sin in the present world, human susceptibility to "natural" tendencies, and the need for spiritual regeneration. As the Book of Mormon declares, "All mankind, yea, men and women, all nations, kindreds, tongues and people, must be born again; yea, born of God, changed from their carnal and fallen [corruptible] state, to a state of righteousness, being redeemed of God, becoming his sons and daughters."[20] Joseph Smith died fifteen years before Darwin's famous treatise was published but would doubtless have found his version of evolution at least consistent with his understanding of human nature. Not metaphysically transmitted sinfulness, but biologically inherited instincts threaten to overwhelm the goodness that originally inheres in the human spirit. "When our spirits took possession of these tabernacles," preached Brigham Young, "they were as pure as the angels of God, wherefore total depravity cannot be a true doctrine."[21] On the other hand, Young acknowledges that "the body is of the earth, . . . and is under the mighty influence of that fallen nature that is of the earth."²² The heritage entailed by material, bodily inheritance, not imputed guilt, is the problem. In this context, the mortal condition is not the unfortunate detritus of the couple Adam's catastrophic decision but, rather, a consequence of entirely natural processes and biological forces that bequeath upon us a fraught inheritance.

This is the direction in which the book of Moses reshapes our understanding of sin. Adam asks the Lord the question that goes to the heart of the matter: "Why is it that men must repent?" It is *not*, the Lord replies, because of inherent depravity or sinfulness. "The Son of God hath atoned for original guilt," Adam is told. And then the Lord explains, "Inasmuch as thy children are *conceived in sin*, even so when they begin to grow up, *sin conceiveth in their hearts*, and they taste the bitter, that they may know to prize the good."²³ This is a remarkable recasting of sin. We are born innocent. We are not conceived in a personal condition of sin; we are conceived, and born, in a world immersed in bitterness, pain, and suffering, and we bear the scars and wounds it inflicts upon us. President Dieter F. Uchtdorf elaborated this point: "Here on earth, our thoughts and actions become encumbered with that which is corrupt, unholy, and impure. The dust and filth of the world stain our souls, making it difficult to recognize and remember our birthright and purpose. But all this cannot change who we truly are. The fundamental divinity of our nature remains."²⁴

We hear in his words a return to the pure gospel taught before the destructive Western theology of sin gained the upper hand. Contemporary with Augustine, in the Eastern Church, Theodore of Mopsuestia was teaching that "the necessity of satisfying the needs of the body—food, drink, and other bodily needs—are absent in immortal beings, but among mortals they can lead to 'passions,' for they are the unavoidable means of temporary survival."²⁵ Slightly later, another Eastern bishop, Theodoret of Cyrus, teaches that "having become mortal, [Eve and Adam] conceived mortal children, and mortal beings are necessarily subject to passions and fears, to pleasures and sorrows, to anger and hatred."²⁶ As the historian John Meyendorff summarizes, there is "a consensus" in these early Eastern Church Fathers "in identifying the inheritance of the Fall as an inheritance . . . of mortality rather than sinfulness, sinfulness being merely a consequence of mortality."[27] The very burden of our corporeal humanity, with all its carnal, selfish, and passional attributes, is very much to the divine purpose behind embodiment, as intended from those first primordial councils.

Joseph taught the primal innocence of humans, but he was under no illusions about their susceptibility to the evil in the world and their capacity to sin. He unhesitatingly acknowledged that "in this world mankind are naturally selfish ambitious & striving to excel one above another."[28] In a Church editorial, he complained that "Satan was generally blamed for the evils which we did, but if he was the cause of all our wickedness, men could not be condemned."[29] Some pain and suffering, in other words, can be laid squarely at our own willful decisions to sin. At the same time, however, Joseph noted that "what many people call sin was not sin & he did many things to break down superstition."[30] Neither guilt nor corruption of the will follows upon the Adamic Fall: they do not define us. The human condition is one of vulnerability to temptation, susceptibility to the natural predispositions of a human body, and a soul still untried and untested in the crucible of mortal existence. When Paul wrote of his fear lest we be "overcome of evil," it was likely the world's pain and suffering, not our personal proclivities, that were his concern.[31] Succumbing to despair, not wickedness, is the temptation of the tenderhearted. In Mormon thought, humans are neither capable of unaided advancement to godliness nor accurately described as depraved. They are agents made free by Christ's Atonement, enticed by darkness while yearning for the light.

We do not dispute that in Christ, we overcome sin, corruption, and death. We nonetheless believe that the effects of privileging words like *reversal* over *advancement*, *corruption* over *woundedness*, and *sin* over *pain* frame our purpose in life with a defeatist posture while doing injustice to God's plan, Christ's nature, and our predicament. In early America, schoolchildren often learned their letters from a single sheet mounted on a wooden tablet, called a hornbook. Today, a children's primer might begin with "A is for apple." But generations of impressionable children began their journey to literacy with the printed phrase, "In Adam's fall, we sinned all." The symbolic import of this historic practice is profound. One could not so much as learn to read, to begin one's schooling, to become socialized into the Christian world of the educated and cultured, without first mastering the foundational sentence of what was supposedly both religious and academic fact: we are guilty, sinful, and fallen as we take our first breath.

The poet Alfred, Lord Tennyson, wrote of his own pained sense of unworthiness, and of the divine response that pierced his soul:

> *The spirit of true love replied;*
> *"Thou canst not move me from thy side,*
> *Nor human frailty do me wrong . . .*
> *So fret not . . .*
> *That life is dash'd with flecks of sin.*
> *Abide. Thy wealth is gather'd in,*
> *When Time hath sunder'd shell from pearl."*[32]

A beautiful illustration of how this reorientation could reshape our self-concept, as well as our interactions with others, comes from an early twentieth-century Russian priest. He wrote, "The smallest particle of good realized and applied to life, a single vivid experience of love, will advance us much further, will far more protect our souls from evil, than the most arduous struggle against sin, that resistance to sin by the severest ascetic methods of chaining the dark passions within us."[33] Joseph spoke to similar effect: "When persons manifest the least kindness and love to me, O what power it has over my mind, while the opposite course has a tendency to harrow up all the harsh feelings and depress the human mind."[34]

CHAPTER 10

THE COLLABORATIVE CHRIST

I do in some small degree participate in the grace that saved me.
—MARILYNNE ROBINSON[1]

*Human progress never rolls in on wheels of inevitability;
it comes through the tireless efforts of men [and
women] willing to be co-workers with God.*
—MARTIN LUTHER KING[2]

We saw in chapter 2 how the tri-theism of the New Testament collapsed into the three-in-one Trinity of the creeds. Catholic and Protestant scholars alike note that with regard to the formulation of "one God in three Persons, . . . among Apostolic Fathers, there had been *nothing even remotely approaching . . . such a mentality or perspective*" (emphasis ours).[3] Another historian notes that the "doctrine of the trinity as it was defined by the great church councils of the fourth and fifth centuries is not to be found in the New Testament."[4]

Joseph Smith restored to Christianity not only the doctrine of Heavenly Parents, but a clear and comprehensible Godhead of three distinct individuals—Father, Son, and Holy Spirit—working collaboratively in the form known in any number of ancient traditions as the

Divine Assembly or Heavenly Council.⁵ Elder M. Russell Ballard has invoked this doctrine in our day to urge that our earthly collaborative efforts should be "patterned after the councils in heaven."⁶ We have tried to show that our Savior's Atonement is more fully understood within this context of a collaborative Godhead rather than as a defense against a sovereign God's wrath. God the Father propounds and directs the everlasting covenant; Jesus offers himself as the Atoning One, the Healer; and the Spirit participates as Comforter, Testator, and Sanctifier.

This is, of course, as it should be. Heaven is not a reward for merit or a repair of an Adamic catastrophe; it is an eternal sociality of celestial beings, existing, striving, and creatively engaging in loving relation. Atonement is primarily about healing the pains and strains of injured relationships incurred en route to that destination, fractures among ourselves as humans and with those gentle Parents patiently working to improve and guide us. The perfect harmony and synergy of a collaborative Godhead is not just a model for our own relationships, but a healing enterprise in which we are invited to participate, to collaborate.

Our invitation to join with the Healer in his atoning work occurs at the same instant we are invited into relationship with him. "As the image and likeness of the Creator, man is a creator too, and is called to creative co-operation in the work of God."⁷ Therefore, in the baptismal covenant of adoption we find both a vertical and a horizontal set of opportunities. As we have seen, in this ordinance of adoption we acquire Christ's name, becoming his spiritual children. But the book of Mosiah makes clear that this parent-to-child bond must grow in concert with its horizontal dimension. As members of the family of Christ, we acquire brothers and sisters, and we acknowledge our responsibilities to them. Alma characterizes these as the threefold covenant to bear one another's burdens, to mourn with those in mourning, and to comfort the comfortless.⁸ Events subsequent to Alma's words demonstrate that within this covenant community, Christ binds himself to honor the same three pledges as his disciples. Struggling under the weight of oppression, Alma's young flock pleaded for heavenly aid. "And it came to pass that the voice of the Lord came to them," invoking the exact language of their covenant. The Healer promised to "ease [their] burdens," "visit [them] in their afflictions," and provide "comfort."[9] Scripture provides no more startling illustration of how literally we are to take Christ's repeated invitations to be fellow laborers, co-heirs, fellow citizens, and friends to aid in the creation of Zion—a genuinely collaborative community, enjoying reciprocity of loving obligation and blessedness.

Christ admonishes us to pick up our cross and to follow him as he labored under the weight of his cross. Like Paul, we all have a heavy load with which we struggle. This is why we are called to a particular type of discipleship—to bear another's burden requires that we kneel beside that person and feel the weight of her or his cross. That may take us to unfamiliar terrain. In a hundred-year-old discourse recently republished by the Church, Emma N. Goddard challenged those working with troubled youth to "enter the trenches of their temptations" in order to help them.[10] Berdyaev expressed this imperative with equal force: "The 'good' do not condemn the 'wicked' to hell and enjoy their own triumph, but descend with Christ into hell in order to free them." Compassion "means sharing the desolateness of our [neighbor, her] sense of being forsaken by God, and there is love."[11] It is in the wastelands of our lives that love is to be given and found. Only then is our shared mourning a genuine compassion, a "shared suffering"; only then does our comforting emerge from a place of empathic knowledge and authenticity.

The baptismal covenant in Mosiah is a poetic canon that trains us to observe, to touch, and to share the cross that weighs down our neighbor. That is what discipleship calls us to do. If we have learned anything as parents, as home and visiting teachers, as friends, and as members who have broken bread and shared testimony and stories with fellow Saints in various places and settings, it is that we all carry crosses, which are almost always invisible to those around us. Bearing our own cross makes it sometimes difficult—if not impossible—to perceive anything beyond our own struggle to move forward. Terryl remembers a time as bishop when a frustrated, overtaxed, and weary single mother came to express her hurt and anger yet again at a ward that had failed to provide the friendship, mentoring, and moral and social support she and her son needed. He remembers responding with sadness that the ward had so many people struggling under the weight of their own crosses that there were not enough Simons of Cyrene.

Then what of the person who is bereft of any companion to walk by her side? What of those instances in which there is simply no one to hear the articulated or unarticulated cries for help? Fiona has a dear friend who suffered an unspeakable atrocity when just a little girl. Geographically isolated as she was, there was no one to hear her cries or to aid her. In order to survive, as many do, she tucked the horror into the depth of her subconscious mind. Still, the effects continued to haunt her, marring all aspects of her life. She suffered a series of further setbacks and abandonments. Even after she became a member of the Church, she continued to bear the psychological trauma bound up in the hidden memory, in addition to single-mother travails. Still, she remained faithful—accepting callings and attending sacrament meetings week after week and year after year. Fiona marveled at her courage and tenacity. There was no evidence of any respite or healing. Yet, still, she came.

Then one day, out of the blue, she approached Fiona with the words: "I have something important to share with you." Disconcerted, in spite of her earnestness, that she should approach Fiona in a location she would never have associated with the sacred, Fiona was nevertheless roused from her discomfort by the following words— words that often precede revelatory experience: "I do not know if I was awake or asleep, . . . but last night the Savior appeared at the foot of my bed. He was weeping. He called me by my name and spoke:

'I am so sorry for your life. I am so sorry for your life,' which, while weeping, he continued to repeat until I awoke the next morning to find my pillow bathed in my own tears." Tears of divine healing. Tears of absolute love. She awoke with the knowledge that in the absence of ministering angels, she learned what few of us experience so profoundly: "Man is never left completely alone, abandoned to his own resources. . . . God is taking part in his life and destiny."[12]

Nothing extraordinary changed in her day-to-day life; she still struggles with the familiar difficulties. Something remarkable, however, had transpired in her soul—she knows the Savior is a co-participant in her suffering, and his image is engraven upon her countenance. Tyler Johnson has evoked a powerful picture, based on his reading of Alma 7, of Christ's "personal act of willing sacrifice wherein the Savior enters into our suffering with each of us one at a time." As he renders this image, "I saw, in my mind's eye," how "in every particular, he suffers with me: each pain, each sin, each sickness, each sorrow. He willingly stays for the duration, feeling each lash I endure with flesh every bit as sensitive as mine. He stays with me, he cries with me, he suffers with me, and, by the end, his empathy for me glows—perfect and complete."[13]

Within our mortal limits, we are asked to imitate his acts of infinite empathy. If we deprive ourselves of sharing the crosses of our fellow pilgrims, we have impeded the only principles by which heavenly society is created. President Spencer W. Kimball stated that "God does notice us, and he watches over us. But it is usually through another person that he meets our needs."[14] John Wesley, whom Brigham Young called "as good [a man] as ever walked on this earth,"[15] preached that "the grand reason why God is pleased to assist men by men, rather than immediately by himself, is undoubtedly to endear us to each other by these mutual good offices, in order to increase our happiness both in time and eternity. And is it not for the same reason that God is pleased to give his angels charge over us? namely, that he may endear us and them to each other."[16] Wesley here approaches Joseph's understanding of eternal sociability. The "great mission" of the Saints was to "organize a nucleus of Heaven," Joseph preached.[17]

Zion-building is not *preparation* for heaven. It *is* heaven, in embryo. The process of sanctifying disciples of Christ, constituting them into a community of love and harmony, does not *qualify* individuals for heaven; sanctification and celestial relationality *are* the essence of heaven. Zion, in this conception, is both an ideal and a transitional stage into the salvation toward which all Christians strive. These outlines of the eternal covenant were clear to the early Church, manifest in cradle Christianity if not in creedal Christianity. According to Tertullian, the first Christians were ridiculed "because we call each other brother and sister," and they believed in the interrelatedness of the human family as a whole. "We are your brothers and sisters as well," he adds. They apparently lived those precepts to a conspicuous degree: "What marks us in the eye of our enemies is our practice of lovingkindness: 'Only look,' they say, 'how they love one another.'"[18] The unprecedented innovation of Christianity was the lived experience of entering into an extended family.

That this family began in the unparalleled bonding and "lovingkindness" manifest in the intimacy of congregational units did not mean, as Tertullian expressed, that a more general body of Christ was not to be sought out, recognized, and cherished. The earliest Eucharistic prayer from the first century captures this yearning: "Even as this broken bread was scattered over the hills, and was gathered together and became one, so let Thy Church be gathered from the ends of the earth into Thy Kingdom."[19] Joseph, in fact, saw the Restoration as the gathering together of just such a capacious church. The idea of a spiritual church that exists alongside, to encompass and eventually transcend the institutional church, was persistently reaffirmed to Joseph in modern scripture. As just one example, section 10 of the Doctrine and Covenants contains a rather remarkable reassurance. The date is April 1829, a year *before* the Church was restored. In this revelation, the Lord refers consistently to *his* Church as something that already exists. The Restoration, he says, will not "destroy that which [my people] have [already] received." "Therefore," he continues, "whosoever belongeth to my church [in 1829] need not fear, for such shall inherit the kingdom of heaven." Those who belong to his Church, he tells us, will receive more light. In his words, a "part of my gospel" will be theirs. But this will not, he repeats reassuringly, "destroy my church, but I say this to build up my church."[20] As Saints, we are called to collaborate in the building of Zion with all those who love God and their neighbor, including so many at present unknown to us, and whom the Lord identifies as "holy men [and women] that ye know not of."[21] Until "all who are suffering torment, whether temporal or 'eternal,' . . . are freed, God's Kingdom cannot come."[22]

Wesley imagined, as did Joseph, that the work of fostering and cementing interconnectedness takes place this side of the veil. The Christ that Joseph taught took the principle of human participation in the grand project of human salvation even further, extending it to generations past and yet unborn. Luther wrote that a Christian should "give [him]self as a Christ to [his] neighbor, just as Christ offered himself to me."[23] The imitation of Christ has generally been taken as a challenge to emulate the life and deeds of Jesus. Luther's analogy goes even further, suggesting that in ministering to a fellow pilgrim, we can function in a comparable role—serving as a conduit of relief or succor, sacrificing our time, means, and energy as "a Christ." Latter-day Saints take the analogy further still by a robust reading of Obadiah, who referred to "saviours [who] shall come up on mount Zion."[24]

Joseph first invoked that scriptural expression in 1841, seeing in it a reference to the Abrahamic promise of a literal seed who would bless "all the families of the earth . . . with the blessings of the gospel."[25] Soon, the expression took on the meaning of participating in the work of vicarious redemption. Mormons often feel the weight of responsibility toward our kindred dead. One may also see the doctrine as a remarkable gift, a holy invitation to be a fellow laborer with Christ, co-participating in his grand designs: "We are to be saviors of men of our brethren to redeem our dead friends and the friends of those who will not save their own friends, . . . until we are all linked together again. For one dispensation will hand in their work after another till the Son Jesus hath them all."[26] We are to collaborate, in other words, in the work of healing and repairing disconnected, damaged relationships in the human family. Berdyaev wrote that "one must help others and do good works, not for saving one's own soul, but for love, for the union of men, for the bringing of their souls together in the kingdom of God. Love for man is a value in itself, the quality of goodness is imminent in it."[27] In the greatest sermon he delivered, C. S. Lewis captured the divine potential we are working to unfold in each other. "It is a serious thing to live in a society of possible gods and goddesses, to remember that the dullest and most uninteresting person you talk to may one day be a creature which, if you saw it now, you would be strongly tempted to worship. . . . Next to the Blessed Sacrament itself, your neighbour is the holiest object presented to your senses."[28]

The future prospect for Latter-day Saints is a continuation of collaboration in a never-ending project of creation, healing, and redemption. In Parley Pratt's description of Joseph's sweeping vision, "men are . . . children of the Gods, and destined to advance by degrees, and to make their way by a progressive series of changes, till they become like their father [and mother] in heaven, and like Jesus Christ their elder brother. Thus perfected, the whole family will . . . continue to organize, . . . redeem, and perfect other systems which are now in the womb of Chaos."[29]

There is yet another sense in which atonement and healing involve collaboration. Our participation requires trusting submission to the Healer's hand. That may be the most difficult part of the entire process. A popular tweet reads, "'Do to others what you would want them to do to you' is a good rule, but treating people how they themselves want to be treated is better."[30] That sounds reasonable enough, and one wonders why the Golden Rule wasn't framed that way to begin with. After all, shouldn't the act of kindness depend on the other person's perception of his or her needs or desires? Actually, not necessarily. That would be true if we all knew what actions and conditions were necessary to our happiness, most conducive to our thriving.

That may seem silly or presumptuous. Silly, because of course I know what makes me happy. And presumptuous, because I certainly don't want you thinking your opinion of what I need is more important than my opinion of what I need. But it is in fact neither silly nor presumptuous to doubt your own opinion about what will make you happy. We are capable of phenomenal feats of rationalization and self-deception. That is why Dietrich von Hildebrand wrote that what matters is not the question, "do we *feel* happiness?" but rather "is the objective situation such that we have reason to be happy?"[31] That sounds rather coldhearted and analytical. However, we all, at times, brush up against the fact that we are not always terribly good judges of what makes for our own flourishing—and that is what Hildebrand is suggesting.

His point is made even clearer if we understand the insight of the philosopher Alisdair MacIntyre, who traces to Aristotle this particular understanding of ethics. Aristotle recognized a "fundamental contrast between man-as-he-happens-to-be and man-as-he-could-be-if-he-realized-his-essential-nature." It is this "essential nature" that is not satisfied by chocolate or prime-time television. And the only proof we need of its reality is our dissatisfaction, alone among life forms, with a purely material existence. We know from experience that we are not satisfied with such paltry prizes, even though we are often distracted by their glitter. Before Christianity was a twinkle in the cosmic eye, the entire occidental philosophical tradition recognized that we carry within ourselves the seeds of a nobler, better self than the one we are today. Therefore, as MacIntyre continues,

"Ethics [or we could say, religion] is the science which is to enable men to understand how they make the transition from the former state to the latter." Here, however, is the real value of this definition: "To say what someone ought to do is at one and the same time to say what course of action will in these circumstances *as a matter of fact* lead toward a man's true end."[32]

We are now moving closer to Hildebrand's statement about "objective" grounds for happiness. For, if we have recognized ethics, or defined religion, as that which moves us from where we are to where we sense we should and could be as free, self-determining human beings, then it is the duty of our religion to shake us out of our complacency. Indeed, true religion should frustrate our plans, reshape our short-term desires, break our habitual ways of responding to what is instinctual and natural in order to move us in the direction of the self that yearns for what Christ calls the more abundant life.[33]

None of this sounds particularly pleasant or terribly appealing. And this is because the purpose of education—moral and mortal—is always to entice us to move beyond the familiar and the comfortable, the pedestrian and the banal, into new, unfamiliar, and uncomfortable places. That is why all our inclinations are to negotiate compromises, invoke unconvincing appeals to our needs, or rationalize our delay in responding to the call of conscience. It also explains why we cannot trust that we are the best judges of what is most needful for our growth toward godliness.

This is the point of one of Mark's most poignant stories in the New Testament, the account of the paralytic lowered by a group of faithful friends to Jesus, in a basket, through a hole in a roof. The story is dramatic and delightful, for it seems a triumph on so many levels.

> And again he entered into Capernaum after some days; and it was noised that he was in the house. And straightway many were gathered together, insomuch that there was no room to receive them, no, not so much as about the door: and

he preached the word unto them. And they come unto him, bringing one sick of the palsy, which was borne of four. And when they could not come nigh unto him for the press, they uncovered the roof where he was: and when they had broken it up, they let down the bed wherein the sick of the palsy lay. When Jesus saw their faith, he said unto the sick of the palsy, Son, thy sins be forgiven thee.[34]

The tale is a triumph, first, of selfless devotion. Who would not envy a man with friends who would carry their disabled companion through dusty streets and packed throngs of onlookers and supplicants to bring him long-sought relief? It is a triumph of imagination and resourcefulness. The friends could have accepted defeat and returned another day, in another setting. But to determine upon a course of action so novel, so daring, as to break down the very roof of a house, secure ropes, and lower their companion into the Lord's presence! It is a triumph of the Lord over his detractors, for he silences those rash enough to protest against his right to forgive sins by what is shortly to follow. And is it not, most of all, a triumph for the paralytic, whose faith is rewarded with the healing he sought? Perhaps not.

It is unlikely that the silent protagonist in this story experienced the whole episode in quite the same way we have imagined. Only those who have suffered years of physical or mental hardship can know the wearying pain, the frustrated hopes, the moments of despair and protracted periods of depression that can accompany the prolonged search for relief. Imagine, if you will, the first rumors that reach the paralytic of the miracle worker from Nazareth, this healer of maladies. With perhaps a mixture of skepticism and desperate hope, he enlists the help of his friends to secure an interview, a moment of consideration from this Jesus. They make the tedious journey. They are, however, unable to penetrate the thick crowds of the devout and the curious; they cannot even make their way into the house where Jesus is speaking. And so the man's hopes fade, only to be rekindled when one of the four suggests a dramatic entry from above. The plan is accepted and executed, the bed descends, and a murmur of grudging admiration for the strangers' chutzpah ripples through the crowd as Jesus pauses in mid-sentence at this unexpected apparition descending by ropes and pulleys. For our weary petitioner, years of hopeless longing now come crashing to a climax; the patient awaits the Healer's hands or words of restoration, only to hear instead this unexpected utterance: "Thy sins be forgiven thee."

We, the readers, know we are in the midst of a great victory for Christ and his message. We know the words are calculated to outrage the haughty and critical among the throng. But what of our poor palsied man? Might he have been disappointed, even bewildered? "This is not what I came for," he may have said to himself. "Such was never my prayer or petition. I have come to the right physician, but he has given me the wrong remedy."

As readers, we rush on to the splendid conclusion; the naysayers are vanquished, the healing words are spoken, "Take up thy bed, and walk,"[35] the miracle effected, and all ends well. Except for one thing. Might the shock of initial disappointment have continued to linger in the mind of the cured man? As he gathered his bed and made his way back to his own home, accompanied by his jubilant companions, was he strangely silent? Did he reflect upon the perplexing sequence of events and the two expressions from the Savior's lips? Did he rest uneasily that night, wondering which of the two were the words he most needed to hear, the words his soul most longed for? Was it physical relief, or was it wholeness or forgiveness he most needed? Or were those just two different forms of the same thing, two different ways of bringing healing to his wounded life?

Our point is not by any means that sin is generally the only source of our suffering. It may often be. Our point, however, and we think Mark's point, is that our deepest healing seldom comes in the ways or modes that we envision. What we think we need to be happy and whole is not always what the Healer *knows* we need to be happy and whole. Solutions that seem obvious to us may be distractions from where the deepest pain lies.

Our niece was recently serving an LDS mission in a rural area of Peru. With her companion, she visited a member and upon departing asked if she knew of anyone who might benefit from a message about the Savior. "Yes," the member replied. "I have a dear friend who has suffered a terrible tragedy. Her young daughter was struck by a motorized cart a few weeks ago. Yesterday the girl passed away. I think the grieving mother needs your message."

The two sister missionaries left with the member's sketch for finding the house, some distance away. As they made their way up the road, they came to a path that was not indicated on their map, yet both felt the prompting to take it. They walked farther. The path led to a group of scattered dwellings on the hillside. They were strongly impressed to approach one door in particular, even though it was not the one indicated in their directions. A woman came to the door in response to their insistent knocking. "We come to you with a message about the Savior," they said. "Would you like to hear it?" The woman immediately burst into tears, said she would, and brought three chairs outside. Before they could continue she explained, weeping, "A short time ago, my husband left me. I am alone with three children and an infant, struggling to provide for the five of us. A few weeks ago, I had a terrible accident. Driving my motor cart, I hit a young girl. I have just learned that she has died."[36] The Great Physician knows where his healing is most needed.

A loving Savior does all he can to help us choose the most fulfilling and most healing pathway; the precepts with which he provides us are for our liberation and not our confinement. It all comes down to trust. "The servant knoweth not what his lord doeth," he tells his disciples, "but I have called you friends."[37] Friends trust each other. One way to find trust in the Healer is in witnessing his susceptibility to human needs. All five Gospel writers (we include the author of Third Nephi in this group) are struck by the way in which personal entreaty can alter his course, change his plans, move him and persuade him to paths he, seemingly, had not intended. In Mark, the Savior declines to bless the child of the Gentile woman. Her persistence dissolves his resistance and he relents, "saying go thy way; the devil is gone out of thy daughter."[38] In John, his heart inclines toward the beseeching Samaritans, and he agrees to "tarry with them: and he abode there two days."[39] In Luke's post-resurrection story, Jesus clearly has in mind to continue beyond Emmaus, but his disciples "constrained him, saying, Abide with us: for it is toward evening, and the day is far spent. And he went in to tarry with them."[40] And in Matthew's account, even the Gadarene demons win his sympathy. "If thou cast us out," they plead, "suffer us to go away into the herd of swine. And he said unto them, Go."[41]

It is in Third Nephi, however, that we find the most tender portrait of a Christ fully vulnerable to human woundedness. "And it came to pass that when Jesus had thus spoken, he cast his eyes round about again on the multitude, and beheld they were in tears, and did look steadfastly upon him as if they would ask him to tarry a little longer with them. And he said unto them: Behold, my bowels are filled with compassion towards you. Have ye any that are sick among you? Bring them hither. Have ye any that are lame, or blind, or halt, or maimed, or leprous, or that are withered, or that are deaf, or that are afflicted in any manner? Bring them hither and I will heal them."[42]

Of course, not all suffering can be alleviated when and how we wish. In such cases, our promise is that our suffering can be sanctified. Gregory of Nazianzus posed a question about Christ's mortal experiences. "Jesus Who Chose The Fishermen, Himself also useth a net, and changeth place for place. Why?" He then ventured an answer: "that He may hallow more places.... He teacheth, now on a mountain; now He discourseth on a plain; now He passeth over into a ship; now He rebuketh the surges. And perhaps He goes to sleep, in order that He may bless sleep also; perhaps He is tired that He may hallow weariness also; perhaps He weeps that He may make tears blessed."[43] That the Creator of the world, the Divine Son, worked a net, slept off his weariness, ate fish and loaves, and wept over Lazarus imbues such human actions with holiness.

Most significant for our healing, perhaps, is our knowledge that by his suffering, he made our suffering holy. As Justin Martyr taught, by "becoming a partaker of our sufferings, he might also bring us healing."[44] This purpose was critical to Christ's Atonement; Enoch was promised that "the blood of the Righteous [would] be shed, that all they that mourn may be sanctified."[45] This principle is implicit in the sacrament of the Lord's Supper. In this weekly ritual, we are eating symbolically the Lord's broken body and drinking his spilled blood. These are emblems of the suffering Christ, and the sacrament prayer is that these emblems of his suffering will be sanctified, made holy to us and in us. As we remember with gratitude his pain and agony, we are at the same time reminded that our own pain and agony are being sanctified. For Latter-day Saints, partaking of this sacrament is an ordinance that unites us in shared and sanctifying suffering. "Through suffering, Christ showed us that our own suffering is worthwhile, and the occasion through which to grow morally by imitating him."[46]

In A. J. Cronin's poignant novel *The Keys of the Kingdom*, a kindly priest persists in his friendship for a rebellious atheist. "I still can't believe in God," he announces near his life's close. "Does that matter now? He believes in you." "Don't delude yourself," the man replies. "I'm not repentant," to which the priest responds, "All human suffering is an act of repentance."[47] In this same spirit, Charles Taylor gives us a piercing insight into the nature of sin: "Our sin is our resistance to going along with God's initiative in making suffering reparative."[48] His observation implies a particularly coherent account of suffering that partakes of our own perspective shaped by the Restoration account of our mortal journey. Our suffering is not punitive, nor is it the spillover of an Adamic rebellion. It was at the very heart of the journey that our Heavenly Parents proposed, and may likely have been the aspect that incited a third of our spirit siblings to reject the mortal estate. As Edward Beecher opined, it was "a discipline of suffering, such as they needed to fit them to be the founders of the universe with God," that appalled and then overwhelmed the indecisive.[49] In those cases and our own, it is—ultimately—the making of divinity, not humanity, that is in play.

We do not fully understand the cosmic law according to which only pain can launch us on the path of celestial growth—only that there is no other way. Participatory suffering weaves the fibers of our heart into those of our children, loved ones, and neighbors—through a shared pain that is the most powerful bonding agent in the eternities. Ritually remembering the Healer's ultimate act of suffering is a powerful means of affirming its sanctifying power in our lives. It reminds us that for us, and for our Healer, "all that we truly esteem, love included, depends in the end on suffering, and on our freedom to accept suffering for another's sake."[50]

In the earliest Church, the Eucharist or Lord's Supper had another purpose, even more primary than drawing our hearts to Christ's suffering. Gregory of Nyssa saw the Eucharist as commemorating "the *glorified* Body of Christ, the seed of immortality."[51] The bread betokened his incarnate body, assumed, according to Byzantine theology, in order "to lead [humanity] to resurrection."[52] Irenaeus was explicit in this regard: "The bread, which is produced from the earth, when it receives the invocation of God, is no longer common bread, but the Eucharist, consisting of two realities, earthly and heavenly; so also our bodies, when they receive the Eucharist, are no longer corruptible, having the hope of the resurrection to eternity."[53] In this beautiful conception, the resurrection is already set in motion—the new life already begins—as we participate in those ordinances that signify our cooperation in God's adoptive purposes.

Finding triumphant as well as tragic echoes in the sacramental emblems is true of Mormonism as well, particularly as the ritual is described in the Book of Mormon. There a recently resurrected Christ institutes the ordinance in the New World. In that account, the Savior commands a multitude to partake regularly of bread and wine "in remembrance of [his] body," with the promise that if they "always remember" him, they will "have [his spirit] to be with [them]."[54] As Kathleen Flake has pointed out, the body to which the New World sacrament points is not a body facing imminent crucifixion but one that is recently resurrected, restored to life—an immortal body "which I have shown unto you," in the Savior's words to a Nephite multitude.[55] For this reason, Mormon practice has particular affinity with the Church Father Ignatius quoted earlier. The Eucharist, he wrote, is the "medicine of immortality," portending a new life already won for humankind. And so the sacrament commemorates Christ's resurrected body, even as it signifies the promise of our own.

CHAPTER 11

The Judging Christ

For God did not send His Son to the world that He may judge the world, but that the world may be saved through Him.
—JOHN 3:17 (YOUNG'S LITERAL TRANSLATION)

I, the Lord, remember [your sins] no more.
—D&C 58:42

The first human emotion unambiguously depicted in the scriptural record is shame. Adam and Eve together hide from God's presence, shielding their very bodies from the gaze of God—and from each other. What might the shame of their nakedness mean in the language of scripture? It may be helpful to consider that we are ashamed primarily before those we love. We can be embarrassed in front of strangers, but the piercing pain of shame is most acute within our circles of intimacy. To be unmasked as a fraud before a spouse, or as a dissembler in front of our child, would be a pain with few parallels. We also suffer shame undeservedly, as when we feel inadequate or unworthy in the face of family, friends, and God. We don't want to disappoint those whose regard we most value. Shame is that disappointment we feel most acutely within a relationship; it is a pain compounded by the gaze of another. Because we yearn for the affection and esteem of those we most love, we experience shame when we feel that we have forfeited such love and regard. Even if we are frankly forgiven by the other, our intractable sense of justice convinces us that we are henceforth not *deserving* of that love or loyalty. We are no longer *capable* of reciprocity, we are no longer *able to receive* that love. This explains the serpent tooth of shame, and why we feel its sting most deeply with those whose love we most cherish.

How much more does this analysis hold true with our Savior. When we feel we have disappointed him by our sin, or poor judgment, or an unfounded sense of nonspecific unworthiness, we think we have alienated him who most deserves our affection, for whose love we most hunger, whose approbation we most desire. The intellectual recognition that his mercy extends to us may help to dissipate the guilt, but not the shame.

Perhaps you have known this experience: you carry for years a low-grade, nagging guilt about a slight you have committed against a loved one. One day, in a moment of particular contrition and sharing, you ask forgiveness for that hurt perpetrated years ago. Your sibling says, with some surprise, "I don't even remember that!" Not only do you relax in sudden relief, happy to know the inflicted pain was less than feared; your relationship is suddenly transformed. Freed of shame, you are now able to relinquish your fear. An invisible barrier has disappeared, a channel has cleared, and now love uninhibited can flow in both directions.

God and Christ are omniscient, and yet the promise is: "He who has repented of his sins, the same is forgiven, and I, the Lord, *remember them no more*."[1] Our Lord is like the mother of Wendell Berry's poem, whose forgiveness is "so complete" that "I wonder sometimes if it did not precede my wrong."[2] He purposely forgets our sins, to extirpate our shame. The act is sublime. Feeling himself to be in a spiritual wilderness, Berdyaev imagined a purer Christianity such as Joseph restored: "Christianity alone teaches that the past can be wiped out; it knows the mystery of forgetting and cancelling the past. This is the mystery of redemption. . . . The endless threads stretching from the past into the future are cut. Therein lies the mystery of penitence and the remission of sins. . . . It is only in and through Christ that the past can be forgiven *and forgotten.*"[3]

It is in the forgiving *and the forgetting* that healing lies. It is not in the quenching of divine wrath or eternal justice that we find the miracle, but in the healing of our wounds. The imagery of Isaiah is quite explicit here. "Though your sins be as scarlet, they shall be as white as snow; though they be red like crimson, they shall be as wool."[4] This mystery of a Christ who heals our wounds and forgets our wrongs steers our understanding of judgment in new directions.

At the end of a discussion about the absolute love of the weeping God of Enoch, a young adult at the back of the room asked, "But what about judgment?" "How do you feel when you hear the word *judgment?*" we asked. "I feel frightened," he said. "I feel fear." Indeed, *judgment* has become a frightful word—with good reason. It is a commonplace of theological understanding, notes one scholar, that "the concept of an eternal hell is based on the assumption of the justice of retributive punishment."[5] "Day of wrath, that day will turn the earth to ash, What dread there will be when the Judge shall come!" intone the lines of Mozart's *Requiem.*[6] It is tragically erroneous to maintain that such is the purpose or intent of judgment. Indeed, Jesus testifies in John's gospel that such is *not* the purpose of Christ's engagement with the human family: "I came not to judge the world, but to save the world."[7] We have, thankfully, left behind much of the medieval Church's imagery of sulfurous pits, the Reformation's language of "total depravity" and "desperate corruption," and Puritan sermons about a spiteful God holding souls over hell like a vicious boy with a spider. Still, Mormon culture has not fully shaken off what Aaron called the "traditions of their fathers, which were not correct."[8]

Christ himself, engaging a woman caught in the very act of adultery, emphasized that judgment does not entail condemnation. "Where are . . . thine accusers?" he asked, before adding, "Neither do I condemn thee."[9] We might do well to note the term he employed here: κατήγορος (kategoros), or accuser, is the very word used elsewhere in the New Testament to refer to Satan.[10] *Satan*, in fact, is the Hebrew word for *accuser*.[11] Accusatory judgment is Satan's role, not Christ's. "We do not know the inmost depths of the human heart; it is revealed only to love. But those who condemn have generally little love, and therefore the mystery of the heart which they judge is closed to them."[12] This may be implicit in the words to Joseph Smith, that "pure knowledge . . . shall greatly enlarge thy soul."[13] It is impossible to know another completely and not love that person deeply.

In the shadow of the rising Nauvoo Temple, a contemporary recorded, "Joseph then delivered unto us an Edifying address showing us what temperance faith virtue, charity & truth was he also said if we did not accuse one another God would not accuse us & if we had no accuser we should enter heaven. . . . He did many things to break down superstition."[14] It seems a curious thing to preach that our forgiveness of another can affect *that other's* salvation as well as ours. Berdyaev confirms this perspective: man must "in the name of Christ forgive his neighbor's sin and evil and help him to free himself from their power. If a man is condemned [by us] as hopelessly wicked, this does not help to liberate or save or improve him. On the contrary, the condemnation ruins him."[15] This is why mercy "is twice blessed; it blesseth him that gives, and him that [receives]."[16]

In the Latter-day Saint conception of salvation, this view makes perfect sense, for two reasons. First, we believe that we are free to choose, and that we will ultimately receive what we choose. That is a core truth of the universe because, as we saw above, that is what Christ's Atonement guaranteed. If "you are merciful unto your brethren . . . ye shall have mercy restored unto you again."[17] Second, as Latter-day Saints, we know we do not *earn* heaven; we *co-create* heaven, and we do so by participating in the celestial relationships that are its essence (and which temple ordinances eternalize). In a very real sense, then, the act of forgiving one another is the healing and constituting of the heavenly sociality we are called to build and to be a part of. It is required that we forgive one another, not as a test of our righteousness but because heaven is simply not possible on any other terms. Then what of judgment?

We need to recover judgment's more benevolent character. The Greek word, κρίνω (krínō), had the original meaning of "to separate," as in "to distinguish." From the opening pages of Genesis to the finale of Revelation, the divine activity has at its heart the ordering of the universe and its inhabitants through a process of differentiation and assessment: earth from sky, land from sea, man from woman—with the resultant verdict of "good." When Adam and Eve partake of the fruit, the divine consequence is that they become "as one of us [the Gods], to know good and evil."[18] These remarkable words tell us that their reborn capacity to judge, or discern, is the next step in their ascent toward divinity. However, this godlike capacity to judge is love-centered.

Compassion grows along the path of discipleship. "The nearer we get to our heavenly Father the more are we disposed to look with compassion on perishing souls to take them upon our shoulders and cast their sins behind our back," taught Joseph.[19] That is a hard thing, but even more daunting is self-forgiveness, accepting that we ourselves are so looked upon by a compassionate Christ, who casts our sins behind his back. Julian of Norwich expresses likewise the belief that there is no "being who can know how much and how sweetly and how tenderly the Creator loves us."[20] The poet William Blake believed our capacity to love was in need of mortal stretching, hence we came to earth "that we may learn to bear the beams of love."[21] It is no easy thing, in our finitude, to comprehend a love that enfolds the cosmos, yet knows us by name. Enoch's soul had to swell "wide as eternity"[22] before he could take in the grandeur of godly compassion—and the experience shook the heavens. Only through a journey that tracked from persecutor to convert to apostle to brutalized and eventually martyred witness, did Paul come to know "that neither death, nor life, nor angels, nor principalities, nor powers, nor things present, nor things to come, nor height, nor depth, nor any other creature, shall be able to separate us from the love of God, which is in Christ Jesus our Lord."²³

Milton, in fact, imagined that Satan's revolt was itself ignited by his incapacity to accept a gift greater than either his merit or his ability to repay.

> *All his good proved ill in me,*
> *. . . . The debt immense of endless gratitude,*
> *So burdensome, still paying, still to owe;*
> *Forgetful what from him I still received,*
> *And understood not that a grateful mind*
> *By owing owes not . . .* ²⁴

In the minds of many, God's love waits upon our worthiness or our response to him—his disposition to bless or love or forgive hangs upon us. The apostles, however, teach a different God. "He first loved us."²⁵ There is perhaps no greater yearning than the human hunger to be known, acknowledged, witnessed. This is the promise held forth in Yahweh's words to Moses: "I know thee. . . . I know thee by name."²⁶ One scriptwriter, wiser than most, understood this. In a rare film that affirms the good of familial relationships, a woman asks an acquaintance, "Why do you think that people get married?" He says, "Passion." She says, "No!" He says, "Why then do people get married?" She replies, "Because we need a witness for our lives. There are a billion people on this planet. What does any one life really mean?" In committed relationships, "you are promising to care for one person . . . to care about them in everything: in the good things, in the bad things, in the terrible things, in the mundane things. All the time! Every day! You're saying, 'Your life will not go unnoticed because I love you and I will notice. Your life will not go unwitnessed because I will be your witness.'"²⁷

The seeds of this desire to be known are there from birth. Among toddlers' first words are "Watch! Look at me!" Self-worth does not come innately. At our deepest core, we seek our place in a web of relationships, and only when we find it do we feel whole and complete and secure. At the most profound level of our being, it is the longing for relationships that motivates us. The Jewish theologian Martin Buber notes how this is most evident with children, who form relationships with imaginary creatures and stuffed animals sometimes even before language takes shape. As he recognizes, "It is not as if a child first saw an object and then entered into some relationship with that. Rather the longing for relation is primary, the cupped hand into which the being that confronts us nestles." The key is that the encounter begins as a "readiness, as a form that reaches out to be filled."[28]

We seek this affirmation in the gaze of the beloved. Darwin marveled at the unfathomable complexity of the human eye, freely admitting that its miraculous powers were reasonably (though not legitimately) seen as a challenge to his theory of evolution: "To suppose that the eye with all its inimitable contrivances for adjusting the focus to different distances, for admitting different amounts of light, and for the correction of spherical and chromatic aberration, could have been formed by natural selection, seems, I freely confess, absurd in the highest possible degree."[29] Perhaps more amazing, even, is the power of the human eye to serve not as the soul's window but as its prism, magnifying, concealing, radiating, or confirming the most profound and powerful vibrations of the heart. It is to the eye we look for approval, for affirmation, for the quiet confirmation that love is here. If that is true, how do we feel and know the Savior's gaze?

In the story of the rich young man, an aspiring disciple asks Jesus what he must do to be saved. "And Jesus said unto him, . . . Thou knowest the commandments, Do not commit adultery, Do not kill, Do not steal, Do not bear false witness, Defraud not, Honour thy father and mother. And he answered and said unto him, Master, all these have I observed from my youth."[30] We know what comes next. Jesus is going to invite the would-be disciple to relinquish his vast wealth and follow him. At this exact moment, however, the young man is caught in that fraught moment of decision, of self-definition, that occurs between the launch of the faith-seeking enterprise and full discipleship. Jesus has not as yet tried the man's heart, nor the depth of his commitment. It is at this precise juncture that Christ commits himself, revealing his own nature and character. In Julian of Norwich's language, "our Lord revealed, most sweetly and most powerfully, his everlasting and immutable love, . . . in the ties that bind us to him, worlds without end."[31] Before discipleship is demonstrated, Jesus manifests his compassion. His absolute love irrupts into the silence that precedes any possible condition of reciprocity or exchange: "Then Jesus beholding him loved him."[32]

We assume that the man declines the invitation to sell all and follow the Christ. However, the end of the story is not given. It may be that after a wrestle, like the young Francis of Assisi, the rich man does relinquish his riches. However, at this juncture of the story as told, Christ's gesture of love seems premature, or one of prescient pity. Perhaps it is neither. What *is* demonstrated conclusively is that the love Christ has for the young man and us is individuated, situational, and absolute. It is not a love in the abstract, and it is manifest without preconditions. In this story, one can see the gaze of our Lord meeting the earnestly entreating eyes of the seeker. Out of the thronging multitudes, this person has sought out Jesus, approached Him, and made his query. Jesus does not answer without first looking upon the soul who has ventured to address him. His gaze apprehends him, holds him—and embraces him.

This is not the love of which some theologians pontificate and speculate, some passionless, eternally present condition of an impersonal, perfect being. It is an active love that precedes mortality and manifests itself in a continual reoccurrence of unhesitating, absolute love. Love happens, as an event, which Jesus feels and experiences. "And Jesus beholding him loved him." Before the man proves his mettle, before he even knows what is in his own heart, "Jesus beholding him loved him." This is the language of human interaction, which most of us have known. Think of returning home from a mission or a stint at college. There you are, coming down the escalator at the bottom of which friends and relatives are waiting. And beholding you, they love you. Or you step off the train for a visit to your best friend or child or spouse. And in that very moment, like a sun emerging suddenly from behind a cloud, beholding her, you love her. In reading these words, we are with the Savior in the moment of his beholding and in the instantaneous irruption of his love.

What this story has shown us is that God does not love us in the absence of, or even in spite of, our struggles or failings. According to Julian's revelation of Christ it does not matter whether we be "foul or clean, we are always . . . in his love. . . . For the blessed comfort which I saw is generous enough for us all."[33] "Love is holy because it is like grace—the worthiness of the object is never really what matters."[34]

It is in this shadow ground of indecision, of yearning and heart-struggle, hope and doubt, that the Lord beholds us, and loves us. And who of us is not in this same no-man's-land, caught as we all are between our initial, probing, tentative steps toward Christ and a life of total commitment and selflessness and faith. In this our own wilderness sojourn, though the end is not yet determined or perhaps even known, we can be assured, Mark seems to suggest, that Christ, beholding us, loves us.[35]

In judgment we will find, as the rich young man did, that we are in a sacred, safe space where love and understanding prevail, allowing us to come to self-knowledge and self-understanding, perhaps for the first time. We cannot overstate the significance of this shift from accusatory judgment and evaluation to judgment as an awakening of self. The clichéd model of judgment portrays us standing before a selection committee to see if we pass muster before the infliction of a penalty or reward. Jacob, however, draws us in a very different direction, emphasizing that we shall come to "a perfect knowledge" of ourselves.[36] Self-knowledge is the precursor to healing and to wholeness. Judgment is the prelude to progress.

C. S. Lewis once noted that "the prayer preceding all prayers is: May it be the real I who speaks."[37] That is the first half of the path of discipleship—seeing ourselves without pretense or illusions. We may find it more satisfying to make excuses for our behavior than to strive for honesty and self-revelation. We come to see ourselves in "a glass, darkly,"[38] a hazy image in a mirror, as a result of our fearful retreat from painful, vulnerable self-knowing.

For most of us, the path to true self-knowledge is a long and hard-fought battle. The prodigal passed through poverty, hunger, and humiliation before "he came to himself."[39] For others, self-knowledge occurs as an abrupt awakening. Alma's coming to himself occurred over three compact days of self-revelation. As we enter the next state of our existence with "that same spirit which doth possess" our bodies now,[40] the process of self-revelation continues, but it does so under the noncoercive ministrations of absolute love. A century before Joseph Smith lived, Emanuel Swedenborg wrote with inspiration of many of those truths the prophet of the Restoration would soon reveal authoritatively. Swedenborg saw in vision a relational and sociable heaven, three degrees of celestial glory, and the preaching of the gospel to the dead.[41] He also understood judgment as a time of profound self-understanding brought about under heavenly influence, preparing the way for further progress. He explained judgment this way: "Every man, as regards his spirit, has exteriors and interiors." By the exteriors, he means the way we present ourselves to the world. It is the self that we create, the identity we fashion, the image we project to others—and often to ourselves. What he calls the interiors of the spirit, by contrast, are what is genuine and authentic, the true essence of our "own will and consequent thought," which are "rarely manifested in the face, speech, and movements . . . ; as a result of this habit man scarcely knows what his interiors are."[42]

Before we are able to progress further in the eternal worlds, we come to a recognition of our divided self and are guided gently to bring the apparent and the authentic selves into harmony. At that point, we are prepared to move forward. Paul teaches such a version of judgment, when he writes to the Corinthians that "being judged, we are corrected by the Lord, that we *not be condemned.*"[43] Judgment *prevents* condemnation, it does not *precede* it. Judgment is an assist in recognizing our true condition in order that we may improve it, not suffer from it. This moment of coming to oneself, Jacob describes as coming to a "perfect [complete] knowledge" of ourselves.[44] Swedenborg describes the process as being "aroused from sleep into full wakefulness, or like one passing from darkness into light."[45]

As most of us are too harsh on ourselves, this will be a step toward greater peace, self-acceptance, and love of self. That is why, said President Dieter F. Uchtdorf, "that Day of Judgment will be a day of mercy and love—a day when broken hearts are healed, when tears of grief are replaced with tears of gratitude, when all will be made right."[46] As our aching hearts and minds are eased of their burdens and our souls are bathed in effulgent light in that great day, then we will "know as we are known," noble and great ones all.[47] As the Lord assured Moroni, affirming the saving value of this self-knowledge, "because thou hast seen thy weakness thou shalt be made strong, even unto the sitting down in the place which I have prepared in the mansions of my Father."[48]

If our progress is to be eternal, then judgment cannot mean the end of growth or transformation. Alma emphasized this life as the day of our repentance because this world is fashioned as an intense seminar in the school of the eternities. Immersed in a world of pain and suffering, burdened with the "heart-ache and the thousand natural shocks that flesh is heir to," bombarded by appeals to our natural instincts, we "strain . . . at particles of light in the midst of a great darkness."[49] If the purpose of this brief interval in our eternal existence is to give us experience of the bitter that we may learn to prize the good, then even those living lives of perpetual desperation have accomplished at least that much. For as Irenaeus taught, consistent with the book of Moses, experiencing both "the good of obedience and the evil of disobedience," humans have a "two-fold experience, possessing knowledge of both kinds, that . . . [they] may make choice of the better things."[50]

This concentrated dose of soul-stretching, as it were, is not the end of the process. "Repentance will be possible . . . even after death," wrote Elder James E. Talmage. To some, he continued, "it may appear that to teach the possibility of repentance beyond the grave may tend to weaken belief in the absolute necessity of repentance and reformation in this life." There is "no reason for such objection," he explains, when we consider that willful neglect here and now will render the process that much more lengthy and difficult in the future.[51] Joseph taught this doctrine very clearly: excepting only those few who will refuse Christ's mercy till the end, man "cannot be damned [stymied in progress] through all eternity, there is a possibility for his escape in a little time."[52] Death is, therefore, a point in eternity "when this portion of the school is out," articulated Brigham Young.[53] Elder Charles Penrose taught in a general conference address that "There are hundreds of thousands who have heard the gospel in the flesh and through fear or folly have not embraced it, having been afraid to come forward and join themselves with this unpopular people; when they pass away from this stage of being into the spirit world [they] will be prepared to receive it when it is being preached among the spirits there."[54]

Our error here, once again, may be in adopting a language of salvation as either/or, as an event that transpires rather than a process that unfolds. It is also here, once again, that the word *healing* may be more useful than *saving*. "Confess with thy mouth" and "believe in thine heart" and "thou shalt be saved," is the formula we find in Paul,[55] and we sense that surely there must be more involved than a one-time gesture of faith. Indeed there is, and one of Christ's most unusual ministrations seems designed to illustrate this point.

In Mark's account, the people at Bethsaida bring to Jesus one who is blind, asking him to heal the man. "And he took the blind man by the hand, and led him out of the town; and when he had spit on his eyes, and put his hands upon him, he asked him if he saw ought. And he looked up, and said, I see men as trees, walking."

The episode is startling. Surely some of the cynical in the crowd must have scoffed at a healing so incomplete, so insufficient. But "after that he put his hands again upon his eyes, and made him look up: and he was restored, and saw every man clearly."[56] Healing seldom comes in an instant, with one decisive choice or one divine ministration. That is a function of our mortal limitations, not the Healer's. Divine mercy, like the sun, "must dazzle gradually or every man be blind."[57]

The novelist Marilynne Robinson also saw judgment in more compassionate terms. She wrote: "The reaction of God to us might be thought of as aesthetic rather than morally judgmental."[58] God wants us to live beautiful lives, devoid of unnecessary suffering. Certainly right and wrong, sin and virtue are indispensable elements. But the point of God's concern about our sin and virtue is that sin is pain, and virtue is happiness. Sin is whatever is crippling, destructive of human relations, whatever distorts or hedges up the way of flourishing. Virtue, on the other hand, is wholeness, the measure of our creation. We are indeed heavy laden, and Christ, the source of healing balm, wishes us to recognize our need for the *Heiland*—the fountainhead of the abundant life, the source of rest from the illusion of self-sufficiency and from the fear of judgment alike. "There went virtue out of him," Luke records, "and healed them all."[59]

CHAPTER 12

THE SAVING CHRIST

And he who created man for love, by the same love wanted to restore man to the same blessedness and even more. . . . Our Creator wished us to be like Jesus Christ our Savior in heaven forever. . . . And God revealed this all most blessedly, as though to say: See, I am God. See, . . . I do all things. See, I never remove my hands from my works, nor ever shall without end. See, I guide all things to the end that I ordain them for, before time began, with the same power and wisdom and love with which I made them; how should anything be amiss?

—JULIAN OF NORWICH[1]

The soul of man—the spirit, had existed from eternity in the bosom of Divinity, and . . . must ultimately return from whence it came.

—JOSEPH SMITH[2]

No loving parent would propose a plan that shuts the door of happiness to any of his or her children. God reminds Job of a time when "*all* the sons of God shouted for joy."[3] Only a proposal that opens the path to salvation for all God's children would be praiseworthy. And that was clearly understood in the early Christian centuries. Morwenna Ludlow has recently written that, "Indeed, in the early Christian Church there were two important streams of eschatological thought: a universalist stream, which asserted that all people would be saved, and a dualistic stream, which stressed the two parallel fates of eternal heaven and eternal hell."[4] The first tradition was represented by Origen, Gregory of Nyssa, his sister Macrina, Maximus the Confessor, and others. Origen saw mortality as the crucial second stage in an ongoing saga of eternal progression. "The saints who depart this life," he wrote, will progress to a

> place of instruction, and so to speak, class-room or school of souls, in which they are to be instructed . . . and are to receive also some information respecting things that are to follow in the future, . . . all of which are revealed more clearly and distinctly to the saints in their proper time and place. If any one indeed be pure in heart, and holy in mind, . . . he will indeed, by making more rapid progress, quickly ascend . . . and reach the kingdom of heaven. . . . And thus he will in order pass through all gradations, following him who hath passed into the heavens, Jesus the Son of God, who said, "I will that where I am, these may be also."[5]

Gregory of Nyssa taught the same consoling truth: "[God's] end is one, and one only; it is this: when the complete whole of our race shall have been perfected from the first man to the last . . . to offer to every one of us participation in the blessings which are in Him."[6]

Here is no automatic salvation, but a process in which, following death, we would move on to a "school of souls" in which the departed will continue to be instructed "by word, reason, and doctrine; by a call to a better course of things," but always "consistently with the preservation of freedom of the will."[7] Any correction would be medicinal and pedagogical—and therefore not of infinite duration. (Like Joseph, Origen rejected the interpretation of *eternal* as "nonending.")[8] Men are educated insofar as they are drawn by love. This was Origen's emphasis: "the redeeming power of God's love and the universal scope of Christ's incarnation and resurrection."[9] These

Greek Fathers championed a God who never shut the door of salvation to their children, here or hereafter.

The tide did not turn decisively against a generous and forgiving God until a few centuries after Origen. "Since about the fifth or perhaps sixth century," Ludlow continues, the idea of an eternal hell "has been overwhelmingly powerful. This dominance was due partly to the theology of Augustine of Hippo: he denied universal salvation with a forcefulness which had a profound influence on both Catholic and Reformed traditions."[10] The limited, exclusive heaven left an undercurrent of bewildered Christians. As the author of the *Clementine Recognitions*, a fourth-century narrative, put the urgent question: "If those shall enjoy the kingdom of Christ, whom His coming shall find righteous, shall then those be wholly deprived of the kingdom who have died before his coming?"[11] The answer for the vast majority of Christian history has been an almost unqualified yes. With the exception of a few righteous patriarchs rescued by Christ's "harrowing of hell" (visit to the spirit world), there was emphatically no salvation for those who died outside or before the Christian dispensation, or for those who rejected or deferred the call to repent.[12]

Alvin Smith, the Prophet Joseph's older brother, died November 19, 1823, from a toxic dose of calomel (mercurous chloride) administered by a physician for a stomach ailment. He was "taken from us in the vigor of life, in the bloom of youth," mourned his father.[13] "A youth of singular goodness of disposition—kind and amiable, so that lamentation and mourning filled the whole neighborhood in which he resided," recalled his mother.[14] Alvin was a pillar of his family, bearing the brunt of physical labor on the farm and working strenuously to build a frame home for his overtaxed parents. But more than that, he was the spiritual center of the home. "I remember well the pangs of sorrow that swelled my youthful bosom and almost burst my tender heart, when he died," recorded his brother Joseph. Later he commented, "It has been hard for me to live on earth & see those young men upon whom we have leaned upon as a support & comfort taken from us in the midst of their youth[;] yes it has been hard to be reconciled to these things."¹⁵

Joseph refused to believe that we could ever be comforted, in this world or the next, separate and apart from those we love. When the principle of baptism for the dead was revealed to him, the great significance he found in the revelation was not the fact that our ancestors could be saved, but that they could be saved *with us*. That was the whole point of Malachi's prophecy, as Joseph taught a few months before his death: temples, priesthood, ordinances—they all existed in order that our relatives "may Come forth in the first resurrection & be exalted to thrones of glory *with us*, & here in is the chain that binds the hearts of the fathers to the Children, and the Children to the Fathers which fulfills the mission of Elijah."¹⁶ The revealed practice of evangelizing and baptizing the dead and performing their temple ordinances for them erased the dominion of hell over all the earth's unbaptized dead. It bridged a gulf that had separated millions of believing Christians from their forebears as well as from the divine family.

The promise made by the Savior is one of unimaginable joy—perfect, untainted, unqualified joy: "And God shall wipe away all tears from their eyes; and there shall be no more death, neither sorrow, nor crying, neither shall there be any more pain."¹⁷ But if God shall wipe away all tears, he can only do so by triumphing over the cause of those tears, which is death's severing of our most intimate family ties and connections. Any joy we savor in the absence of our loved ones is a partial joy, a fractured joy. Heaven apart from those we love is just hell by another name. Joseph said as much: "let me be resurrected with the Saints," he said to his people in Nauvoo, "whether I ascend to heaven or descend to hell, or go to any other place."¹⁸

Clearly, this leaves us in a bit of a quandary. We believe in a real, literal heaven, and that families (and the whole web of kin and friends Joseph called "sociality") can continue forever. Heaven isn't a place we enjoy with other people; heaven *is* eternal companionship with other people. We also believe in agency and personal accountability. As the first verse of the hymn Emma chose to inaugurate the 1835 hymnbook teaches, "Know this, that ev'ry soul is free To choose his life and what he'll be; For this eternal truth is giv'n: That God will force no man to heav'n."[19] So how do we resolve this dilemma? How can we reconcile a familial heaven with the freedom to reject heaven? We believe we have a gospel wherein hope shines more brightly than we have fathomed, because we have a Savior whose power we have not fully understood, whose plans to heal and redeem extend beyond our mortal view. In this chapter, we hope to retrace a way of making sense of the apparent contradiction between a shared heaven and individual freedom. We will follow this perspective from its roots in the scriptures, through Joseph and other Mormon leaders, up to the present day.

God's reputation has suffered wild pendulum swings throughout Christian history. As we have surveyed, we find the sovereign deity of vengeance and wrath, and we find at the other extreme an indifferent God who will "beat us with a few stripes" and then award us all heavenly bliss.[20] To use another analogy, some have seen God as a stern schoolmaster. He sets the standards, we take the test, and few of us pass. Only occasional A's are handed out, while for most of us, slack and mediocre as we are, a perpetual detention is our destiny.

At the other end of the spectrum, some protest that the only alternative is a saccharine-steeped schoolmarm of a God who indulges her students, pats them sweetly on the head, and gives everyone an A in the end. This is the God of cheap grace, who tells us to eat, drink, and be merry, and expect at most a light caning before we are automatically saved in the end. In fleeing the God of wrath, some have found refuge in this version of the ever-indulgent God.

These options constitute a false dichotomy. We should not think they are the only alternatives. In this book, we are arguing for a third way, because our scriptures and our prophets alike have suggested both views are wrong. We believe our Lord is, rather, the persistently patient master teacher; he is the loving tutor who, devoted to his students, remains with us, staying after class for extra lessons, giving us individualized attention, practicing sums again and again, late into the night, for as long as it takes—until we master the material. And we are transformed in the process by his "long-suffering, by gentleness and meekness, and by love unfeigned; by kindness, and pure knowledge."[21]

This is the Christ of the everlasting covenant, who "is . . . not willing that any should perish."[22] This is the Christ who says, "I have graven thee upon the palms of my hands."[23] This is the Healer who promises, "I will never leave thee, nor forsake thee."[24] "'Make no mistake,' He says, 'if you let Me, I will make you perfect. . . . Whatever it costs me, I will never rest, nor let you rest, until you are literally perfect.'"[25] This is the true meaning of Christ's words in the Beatitudes, "be ye therefore perfect."[26] For *perfect*, as rendered in the original Greek text (*teleios*) or in the German Bible that Joseph called "the most correct" (*vollkommen*), means whole, complete, or having reached its goal or end.[27] And the original verb is in the future tense. "Therefore [that is, by following the path I am proposing] you *shall* be whole and complete," is, indeed, a strictly literal rendering of the passage.[28] We should read Christ's words as expressing his hope, his wish—even his promise—that we will eventually fill the measure of our creation, *become* complete and whole, as part of a process he is overseeing and guiding as our Shepherd and Healer.

Some have mistaken such descriptions of God's long-suffering for an automatic salvation. Elder David A. Bednar explained that the sanctity of agency means the cost of salvation will always be the same: repentance—or change of heart, obedience, and transformation. As he wrote, "Some members of the Church [believe] that wayward children unconditionally receive the blessings of salvation because of and through the faithfulness of parents." However, "The 'tentacles of Divine Providence' described by Elder [Orson F.] Whitney may be considered a type of spiritual power, a heavenly pull or tug that entices a wandering child to return to the fold eventually. Such an influence cannot override the moral agency of a child but nonetheless can invite and beckon. Ultimately, a child must exercise his or her moral agency and respond in faith, repent with full purpose of heart, and act in accordance with the teachings of Christ."[29] A *pull*, a *tug*, an *enticement, invite, beckon*. In these words, we hear an echo of the original promise, "I . . . will *draw all* men unto me."[30]

Like the authority to administer the institutional Church, which is predicated upon noncoercive principles of love and persuasion, the ability to save and redeem the human family relies upon love's irresistible pull. The model for this salvific priesthood is the power by which the Great High Priest effects his Atonement; he exemplifies noncoercive love as that which binds all humans in perfect at-one-ment: "in him all things hold together."[31] Scripture is emphatic that Christ's atoning sacrifice is efficacious by virtue of this draw, the pull, the attractive power it exerts upon our hearts. If "every knee shall bow to" Christ and "every tongue" confess him,[32] LDS scripture suggests it will be a joyful, grateful, voluntary bow, in consequence of the vulnerability of the Savior, a God given to weeping over and in solidarity with the misery of his children, and not in consequence of his active demand. His power is a noncoercive power: "He layeth down his own life that he may draw all men unto him. Wherefore, he commandeth none that they shall not partake of his salvation."[33] As he confirmed in his own voice, "I ha[ve] been lifted up upon the cross, that I might draw all men unto me."[34]

These words emphasize salvation as an invited response rather than a pressured choice or foregone conclusion. "Men are free according to the flesh . . . free to choose liberty and eternal life," the Book of Mormon emphasizes.[35] As the Lutheran minister Dietrich Bonhoeffer put the same principle: "The God of the Bible . . . wins power and space in the world by his weakness," by which he means his vulnerability.[36] For Joseph, God's dominion over the souls of men, like that of exalted beings over each other, is one that "without compulsory means . . . shall flow unto thee forever and ever."[37]

In the Garden of Gethsemane, Christ bore the brunt of the Atonement in solitude, without even his closest friends to witness and sustain him—a solitude mitigated only by the comforting presence of the ministering angel. The final manifestation of Christ's absolute love, however, had to be a public sacrifice, that the perfect offering might be witnessed, and therefore engulf us and transform us. The Roman centurion is emblematic of all so redirected when, stunned by the irruption of absolute love, he could not help but exclaim: "Truly this man was the Son of God."[38] Our healing, our saving, is never with compulsion—never without cost, but never without choice. As Dorothy Sayers wrote, "The perfect work of love demands the co-operation of the creature."[39] The Tutor's patience, however, is everlasting.

We do not find here a God demanding our obedience to his sovereign law so that we may please him and receive his approbation. We encounter a loving Christ beseeching us to change our hearts that we may be healed of our maladies and live life more abundantly. In any case, "salvation cannot be bought with the currency of obedience; it is purchased by the blood of the Son of God," President Dieter F. Uchtdorf reminds us.[40] If we "see obedience as an end in itself, rather than a means to an end," we have misunderstood how the Atonement works.[41]

Nikolai Berdyaev taught the same principle:

> A false interpretation of "good works" leads to a complete perversion of Christianity. "Good works" are regarded not as an expression of love for God and man, not as a manifestation of the gracious source that gives life to others, but as a means of salvation and justification for oneself, as a way of realizing the abstract idea of the Good and receiving a reward in the future life. "Good works," done not for the good of others, but for the good of one's soul, are not good at all.

Where there is no love, there is no goodness. Love does not require or expect any reward, it is reward in itself, it is a ray of paradise illumining and transfiguring reality.[42]

One historian of Christianity saw this misdirection occurring within a few generations of Christ's ministry. Already "with the Apostolic Fathers . . . the actions and dispositions are wholly confused,—actions right and wrong pushing their way more and more into the foreground of the code, and obedience and conformity taking the place of enthusiastic [love of Christ] as the basis of Christian life."[43]

Only when we understand the legitimate motivation for righteous striving can we understand the ground for, and find motivation for, our own repentance. This is repentance as Paul defined it for the Romans: "Do not be conformed to this world, but be transformed by the renewing of your minds, so that you may discern what is the will of God—what is good and acceptable and perfect."[44] Or as the original might be more fully rendered, "Do not allow yourself to be shaped and fashioned by the world in which you find yourself, but be rebirthed in mind and will [*anakainosei tou noos*], that you may sample firsthand through trial and error [*dokimadzein*] what is God's desire for you: the Good, the well-pleasing, the full measure of your creation [*teleion*]."

Paul's words hark back to that moment in the Garden when the entire plan of human embodiment is distilled to its essence: we are placed on earth to prove, that is, to experience, be exposed to and sample, the sweet and the bitter. This, so that we may learn to prize, value, and embrace the good, the true, and the beautiful as our Heavenly Parents have (and precisely as Eve chose: for she recognized in the tree what "was good . . . pleasant to the eyes, and [desirable] to make one wise").[45]

Our task on earth is to resist the conforming of our spirit to our natural environment with its allures and distractions, and to shape our affections, inclinations, and desires in the mold shown us by the

Savior. This is repentance: a conscious choice, born out of contraries, to be shaped and directed into a genuine spiritual begetting after the image of God, in accordance with the seed of divine potential in all of us. This phrase, "discern . . . the will of God," or "sample . . . God's desire for you" echoes the moment when Adam and Eve had "become as" gods, knowing, that is, *discerning*, good and evil, and embarked upon their spiritual journey of choosing the good. And that is also God's *will* for us, because God's motive behind the eternal covenant is that we might accept his invitation to be made like unto our Heavenly Mother and Father. ("Our highest aspiration is to become like our Heavenly Parents," Elder Dallin H. Oaks reminds us.[46]) Hence, God's pained lament to Enoch, confirming unto man "his agency; And unto thy brethren have I said . . . that they should love one another, and that they should choose me, their Father; but behold, they are without affection, and they hate their own blood."[47]

Elihu had taught of such divine motivation when he asked of Job, "If thou sinnest, what doest thou against him? or if thy transgressions be multiplied, what doest thou unto him? If thou be righteous, what givest thou him?"[48] These were paradigm-shifting questions that, tragically, did not seem to register in the religious world then or since. Elihu was clearly and emphatically emphasizing that God does not seek our repentance or righteousness for *his* own glory, or deter our wickedness for *his* own sake. He seeks our repentance for *our* sake. Centuries-long, abject submission to a sovereign God was predicated on the continuing myth that our sole existence is to promote his glory. Paul Ricoeur notes of Friedrich Nietzsche that in the wreckage of his devastating critique of Christianity, "we are henceforth unable to return to a form of moral life which would consist merely of submission to the commandments of a . . . supreme will."[49] As President John Taylor said more simply, decrying that version of Christian worship, "I cannot, will not be a slave. I would not be slave to God! . . . I'd go at His behest; but would not be His slave."[50]

This the Prophet Joseph clearly taught: God "never has, he never will, institute an ordinance, or give a commandment to his people that is not calculated in its nature to promote that happiness which he has designed, and which will not end in the greatest amount of good and glory to those who become the recipients of his law and ordinances."[51] This is the selfless Christ of absolute love reclaimed by the Restoration. "The old lives will not be lived again," as one wise minister noted.[52] Edward Farley reminded us that the seraphim Isaiah saw at the throne of God did not address God as "nice, nice, nice," but as "holy, holy, holy."[53] Our Heavenly Parents dwell in everlasting burnings, and we cannot be purified as they are without passing through the refiner's fire. Christ, however, will be tireless in his efforts to bring us to where the divine family is. For the love of Christ does not

> . . . [alter] when it alteration finds,
> Or bend with the remover to remove,
> . . . It is an ever-fixed mark
> That looks on tempests and is never shaken;
> It is the star to every wandering bark.[54]

Writing far out of the mainstream in Joseph Smith's day was Alexander Galbraith, who urged that we need to see God not as "a Being all fury and vengeance," but "in his true character of a parent,—'The Lord God merciful and gracious, long-suffering and slow to anger, who forgiveth iniquity, transgression and sin,' and hath no pleasure in the death of the wicked; and who is kind unto the unthankful and the evil, and whose tender mercies are over all his works. Thus should the character of Deity be represented to the world."[55] As the hymn sung by Latter-day Saints testifies, "The very foes who slay thee have access to thy grace."[56] Joseph, at the same time, was preaching to dubious Saints that "Our heavenly Father is more liberal in His views, and boundless in His mercies and blessings, than we are ready to believe or receive."[57] In other words, the absolute love our Savior offers us is—literally—inconceivable. Many of the early Latter-day Saints, to whom Joseph revealed his vision of a salvation for all, apostatized.[58] Our difficulty in grasping this generosity, or what the Doctrine and Covenants refers to as our reluctance to be "willing to receive,"[59] seems to be the principal point of the Old Testament book of Jonah. As a seventeenth-century Cambridge philosopher framed the moral, "Neither can the Soul of man behold God, unless it be Godlike."[60]

The Jonah Complex

A zero-sum game is one in which there is a fixed number of resources, and one can only acquire more if someone else receives less. Any benefit won by me can only come at a cost to you. Status, for instance, works like that. As the political theorist Francis Fukuyama writes, "One person's recognition can only come at the expense of the dignity of someone else; status can only be relative. In contests over status, there are no win-win situations."[61] Happiness is not a zero-sum game, but our telestial instincts lead us to act and think as if it were—as if happiness were just another form of status.

Human psychology seems indelibly conditioned to measure our well-being by comparison with our neighbor. Part of this is unavoidable. Wealth and poverty are relative terms; what was rich in twelfth-century England would be very poor indeed in twenty-first-century American suburbia. To a disappointing degree, we similarly assess our own happiness by measuring our conditions and circumstances against those of others. What makes me feel rich or fortunate or successful is not an absolute quantity; it is more often the sense that I am rich*er* or *more* fortunate or *more* successful than my neighbor or colleague. We often reinforce this logic at the dinner table. Telling a child to be grateful he has Brussels sprouts when the Sudanese don't have anything to eat probably won't really help him finish his vegetables. And it sends a dismal message: that we can feel better, happier, more appreciative of our life only if we see our happiness as defined by better circumstances than our neighbors'. It's also a dangerous message because of where it takes us. If happiness, well-being, or blessedness depends on a ranking of privilege or resources or comparative circumstances, then what of heaven?

We feel innately there should be a correlation between our worth and our reward. Before we can even put language to the intuitive concepts we feel, we sense a value we learn to call "fairness." The youngest child will notice if you do not put the same number of scoops into each cone. Unless you managed an A on your report card while I received a B, or you cleaned your room while I didn't, then—and only then—is a distinction not only permissible but expected. It's worth asking what we mean by this tenaciously held concept of fairness, since it has such a powerful pull on us. We like to think that it is another way of speaking of what is just, as we indicated in our discussion a few chapters back. And it has something to do with the connection between choice and consequence. We should get what we deserve, by which we mean, we should get what we earned, qualified for, or *chose*. There should be a clear logic that connects our actions to our reward, and when those two are in sync, when one leads neatly and predictably to the other, we feel we have witnessed fairness—justice. Fairness, then, has to do with a fittedness of what we choose to what follows. But a complication enters the picture at this point. None of us really complain if we receive *more* than we earned, qualified for, or deserved. We are aggrieved, however, if someone *else* receives more. But why should we be? If there is enough for everyone to have their two scoops, why do we resent those who didn't "deserve" theirs? If we don't complain when we receive more than we earned, when the vending machine gives us more than we paid for, when our garden produces more than our efforts predicted, or when we live longer than our habits qualified us to, then perhaps we are not really as concerned about fairness and justice as we thought.

If we resent it when others receive more than their just desserts, it may be because we feel that our happiness is somehow compromised, cheapened, diluted, if our reward isn't *greater* than the other, undeserving, person's. This is in fact selfishness masquerading as high-minded virtue. It is particularly tragic when this propensity infiltrates religion, as it has done historically. Indeed, Thomas Aquinas believed any happiness we felt in heaven was dependent on the fact that most people were consigned to hell. Their suffering was an actual factor in the happiness of the few who were saved: "In order that the happiness of the saints may be more delightful to them and that they may render more copious thanks to God for it, they are allowed to see perfectly the sufferings of the damned."[62] The Anglican William Dawes also felt that the eternal suffering of the wicked gave the saved "a motive to be 'still more sensible' of their own felicity."[63] This rationale persisted into the early nineteenth century: "God knowing that his *little flock* cannot *be happy* any longer than *while they see the misery of the wicked,* . . . the destruction of hell would be the destruction of heaven."[64] Those are disturbing ideas. But is that mentality subtly at work in our own religious understanding?

From the foundations of the world, the Healing Christ anticipated our pervasive predilection to strive for distinction, pegging our happiness to relative rank and position. He knew, however, that such striving cannot be part of our heavenly quest. That is why both the Old and New Testaments forewarned us about the pettiness and smallness of heart cleverly disguised as principle. The small-heartedness of the prodigal's elder brother is familiar to all. "Thou hast killed for [my undeserving brother] the fatted calf."[65] More pointedly, the Savior chastises the jealous workers, who dutifully put in their hours and receive their pay but then grumble that "These last have wrought but one hour, and thou hast made them equal unto us."[66] What moral could those dutiful but ungenerous characters convey, if not a warning about our own "littleness of soul," to use the Lord's language,[67] when we discover, to our surprise, how generously heaven is populated? Even more forceful, however, is the story that unfolds not with a spoiled elder child or hired laborers, but with a prophet called of God.

THE SAVING CHRIST

The story of Jonah is one of the most powerful, beautiful stories in the Old Testament. It is, however, remembered for all the wrong reasons. Jonah's reluctance to accept his mission call takes more dramatic direction than most stories of prophets and missionaries. But his hesitation is both understandable and a familiar pattern. In the eighth century BC, Assyria was a formidable empire, and its capital, Nineveh, was not a welcoming place. Criminals and others meeting the king's displeasure could be executed by the most sadistic methods ever practiced (including impalement and flaying); entering the city to call the ruler to repentance was not an activity a sane individual was likely to undertake. Moses pleaded verbal inadequacy, Enoch his youth, and Isaiah his unclean lips; Jonah did the reasonable thing and fled. We all know the story of his ingestion by the "large fish"—there is no place to hide from the call of the Lord. But the greater lesson is still in Jonah's future. Jonah is readily persuaded by his ordeal. He returns to his appointed task, enters into the city, and preaches. More astonishingly, the king and his people all repent.

At this point in the narrative, the focus returns to Jonah. We have learned of the irresistibility of God's call, of the miraculous preservation at sea, and of the converting power of the Word. What remains, however, is a question that cuts much closer to home. Only at the story's conclusion do we learn the provocative and ultimate question it is meant to pose: What is our personal response in the face of unfathomable compassion? For Jonah had prophesied the utter destruction of Nineveh. Significantly, he did not make his prediction conditional. Apparently, he never considered the possibility that the king would actually alter his behavior. And so he had said quite simply, "Yet forty days, and Nineveh shall be overthrown."[68] To Jonah's utter amazement, however, the king and all his subjects did repent: "God saw their works, that they turned from their evil way; and God repented of the evil, that he had said that he would do unto them; and he did it not."[69]

It is here we come to the essence of the scriptural story. God is so moved by the vast sea change in the people of Nineveh's behavior that he withholds their intended destruction and spares the lives of "sixscore thousand persons." At this point, not only does Jonah fail to rejoice, he is "displeased . . . exceedingly" and "very angry." The entirety of the story has led up to this one question: What do we feel when we see a person receive more by way of blessedness and mercy than he or she "earned" or "deserved"? How do we respond to an overflowing grace? How fit are our hearts to encompass God's gift? As mentioned earlier, Enoch's heart had to swell "wide as eternity" to be a partaker of the divine nature.[70] Do our hearts yet yearn for such generosity? Jonah is the only book in holy scripture to end with a question. It is a question that is not rhetorical, and that burns to this day: "Should not I spare Nineveh?"[71]

This History of an Idea

A contemporary of Joseph Smith, Charlotte Haven, found the Prophet's Nauvoo sermons full of hope and optimism, recuperating the legacy of Christianity's founding fathers. A spirit in the lowest kingdom, she recorded him as saying, "constantly progresses in spiritual knowledge until safely landed in the Celestial."[72] Joseph deliberately represented this process in the temple endowment. Brigham Young was exactly in line with Joseph's thinking. He was teaching in 1855 that those who fail to secure exaltation by the conclusion of their earthly probation "would eventually have the privilege of proving themselves worthy & advancing to a Celestial kingdom but it would be a slow progress."[73] The prophet Lorenzo Snow bore fervent testimony to this principle: "You that are mourning about your children straying away will . . . get all your sons and daughters in the path of exaltation and glory. This is just as sure as that the sun rose this morning over yonder mountains."[74] Later in the century, B. H. Roberts said the ministry alluded to in each kingdom seemed meaningless "unless it be for the purpose of advancing our Father's children along the lines of eternal progress."[75]

THE SAVING CHRIST

Elder James E. Talmage wrote in the first edition of the Church-published *Articles of Faith*, "advancement from grade to grade within any kingdom, and from kingdom to kingdom, will be provided for. . . . Eternity is progressive."[76] He later elaborated, no man will be detained in the lower regions "longer than is necessary to bring him to a fitness for something better. When he reaches that stage the . . . doors will open and there will be rejoicing among the hosts who welcome him into a better state."[77] Slightly later, President Joseph F. Smith taught that "there is a time after this mortal life, and there is a way provided by which we may fulfil the measure of our creation and destiny, and accomplish the whole great work that we have been sent to do, although it may reach far into the future before we fully accomplish it. Jesus had not finished his work when his body was slain, neither did he finish it after his resurrection from the dead, although he had accomplished the purpose for which he then came to the earth, he had not fulfilled all his work. And when will he? Not until he has redeemed and saved every son and daughter of our father Adam that has or ever will be born upon this earth to the end of time, except the sons of perdition."[78]

A counselor in the First Presidency, J. Reuben Clark Jr., testified of his belief that we do not "seal our eternal progress by what we do here. It is my belief that God will save all of His children that he can: and while, if we live unrighteously here, we shall not go to the other side in the same status, so to speak, as those who lived righteously; nevertheless, the unrighteous will have their chance, and in the eons of the eternities that are to follow, they, too, may climb to the destinies to which they who are righteous and serve God, have climbed."[79] It will take "work and labor," as President Snow said. No one will proceed automatically or under compulsion, as Elder David A. Bednar taught.

It is important to note that none of these views resembles the cheap, automatic salvation taught by the anti-Christ Nehor, the "no need to fear or tremble" (or keep the commandments) since

Christ has already "redeemed all men," school of thought.[80] Only "that which is governed by law is . . . perfected and sanctified by the same."[81] Our commitment to keep heaven's precepts fits us for salvation. The time it takes to learn them will vary from individual to individual. Nor are any of these leaders saying we will all be saved "in [our] sins" (the anti-Christ Zeezrom's mistake[82]). Rather, repentance—the changing of the heart—will bring us to "a fitness for something better," as Elder Talmage taught. Finally, no quick fix at the end of life will suffice. ("Ye cannot say, when ye are brought to that awful crisis [like Korihor], that I will repent."[83]) Because as Amulek taught, we will emerge on the other side of the veil with the very same disposition with which we left this one, and time is the necessary requirement for change.[84] As President Joseph F. Smith testified, Christ's work is not completed upon our passing. Like the ever-patient, ever-persistent, ever-loving Tutor, the Savior does not consider his work completed until his words and actions find a way to permeate the core of each person's wounded heart. "Therefore, he giveth this promise unto you, with an immutable covenant that they shall be fulfilled; and all things wherewith you have been afflicted shall work together for your good."[85]

However, the question may be asked: is this life not the time for repentance? Of course this life is the time to repent, for at least three reasons. First, in premortal councils this was the time of probation agreed upon by us to occur between birth and death. Earth life is apparently deliberately constructed in terms of oppositions and conditions most conducive to our spiritual formation. This is the time for which we planned, prepared, and waited. We will never again encounter this particular alignment of the stars, so propitious for our advancement toward godliness. Second, repentance deferred is repentance made more arduous. As the old man admonishes a stubborn Dr. Faustus, habit can become identity. Change is easier, he tells the magus, "if sin by custom grow not into nature."[86] Repentance deliberately deferred, wrote Talmage, is postmortal repentance made more

THE SAVING CHRIST

difficult. Third, "Wickedness never was happiness."[87] If we "consider on the blessed and happy state of those that keep the commandments,"[88] it is immediately clear why now is the time to let our hearts be remolded and our souls sanctified. No sin is without pain. Now is clearly the time to commence the abundant life, to strive to open ourselves to the joy and peace to which Christ invites us.

Doors that never close do not suggest that salvation is automatic. And to say the door is never closed is a far cry from saying there is no doorkeeper at the entrance, no preparation needed. The price of admission is a broken heart and contrite spirit. "Come," the Healer invites. "Come, my brethren, every one that thirsteth, come ye to the waters; and he that hath no money, come buy and eat; yea, come buy wine and milk without money and without price."[89]

Eternity is a long time. Even for the righteous, "it will be a great while" after we have passed through the veil before we know and practice the principles of exaltation.[90] It may be human weakness to confuse an open door with automatic admission. This—and differing opinions on the subject—could explain why in recent years, the Latter-day Saint leadership has balanced faithfulness to Joseph's original liberality with concern for the spiritual slackness a misunderstood long-suffering could invite. The Church leadership has officially declared that the question of eternal progression and movement through the kingdoms is not a resolved point of doctrine. "Some of the Brethren have held that it was possible in the course of progression to advance from one glory to another, invoking the principle of eternal progression; others of the Brethren have taken the opposite view. But as stated, the Church has never announced a definite doctrine on this point," declared two First Presidency statements in the modern era.[91] Just as some scriptures and leaders indicate the promise of eternal repentance, some scriptures and leaders suggest a more permanent judgment at some point. Section 76 of the Doctrine and Covenants indicates that inhabitants of the telestial world cannot enter "where God and Christ dwell . . . worlds without end."[92] That concluding phrase, *aionos ton aionon* in Paul's original language, has convinced some readers of a more permanent, final state. Joseph Fielding Smith, Bruce R. McConkie, and Spencer W. Kimball, among others, felt those words suggested an eternity without the possibility of progressing from lower kingdoms to higher ones (which is why affirmation of the principle was dropped from subsequent editions of Talmage's work). And that may be the case. As we have seen, however, from Joseph to the present, others did not find such words referred to permanent damnation. As Joseph learned and recorded in his reworking of Genesis, *Eternal* is one of God's names or titles: "Behold, I am God; Man of Holiness is my name; Man of Counsel is my name; and Endless and Eternal is my name."[93] The Lord reiterated this point to Joseph in section 19: "eternal" punishment is not endless punishment. "It is not written that there shall be no end to this torment, but it is written endless torment. Again, it is written eternal damnation . . . that it might work upon the hearts of the children of men."[94] Together these two verses suggest that, daunting vocabulary notwithstanding, God's underlying concern is on the educative transformation of the heart. There is deliberate and divine purposefulness, in other words, in the ambiguity of scriptural references to eternal damnation. With God as with mortals, patience and long-suffering are too easily construed as indulgence, and infinite grace too easily misunderstood as cheap grace.

Like "eternal," so is the expression "worlds without end" of ambiguous meaning. Greek scholars note that the fraught expression can suggest "prolonged time or eternity," or "prolonged but not unending time," just as Joseph learned was true of "eternal."[95] Joseph Smith himself was surprised to learn that section 76 did not teach a binding judgment in the way he first understood it to. The terrestrial world, he read, comprised those "who died without law . . . who received not the testimony of Jesus in the flesh, but afterwards received it."[96] His brother Alvin, who died in Joseph's youth, would have been in that category—or so Joseph assumed. Hence his happy shock when, in 1836, through spiritual eyes he saw his brother in the celestial kingdom, "And marveled how it was that he had obtained an inheritance in that kingdom, seeing that he had departed this life before the Lord had set his hand to gather Israel the second time, and had not been baptized for the remission of sins."[97] We cannot say for sure, but one possible inference from Joseph's experience, which his subsequent remarks support, is that Alvin did indeed inherit a terrestrial kingdom as described in section 76, but his progress did not end there.

And thus we find ourselves aligned with James E. Faust, who acknowledged the ambiguity of this great issue, but came down on the side of hopefulness. "I recognize that now is the time to prepare to meet God," he said, affirming the words of Alma, but then asked:

> If the repentance of the wayward children does not happen in this life, is it still possible for the cords of the sealing to be strong enough for them yet to work out their repentance? . . . Mercy will not rob justice, and the sealing power of faithful parents will only claim wayward children upon the condition of their repentance and Christ's Atonement.

And he concluded:

> There are very few whose rebellion and evil deeds are so great that they have sinned away the power to repent. . . . Perhaps in this life we are not given to fully understand how enduring the sealing cords of righteous parents are to their children. It may very well be that there are more helpful sources at work than we know. I believe there is a strong familial pull as the influence of beloved ancestors continues with us from the other side of the veil.[98]

The long-suffering of ever-patient Heavenly Parents invites two questions. Does there not come a time when it is too late, when God does shut the door? And how do we know whether those who now reject the light will someday want to change? Elder Robert D. Hales pleaded with parents in an area conference, "Never, never, shut the door of your heart to any of your children."[99] We can hardly presume that God's prophets are enjoining us to a degree of persistence, hopefulness, and readiness to forgive that exceeds our Heavenly Parents'. And we can, in fact, hear in these words an echo of the Christ who promises, "I will never leave thee, nor forsake thee."[100] How can we presume to put limits to what the Savior has called an eternal love and absolute commitment? Paul knew better, testifying that nothing and no one "shall be able to separate us from the love of God, which is in Christ Jesus our Lord."[101] George Q. Cannon taught that "God will never desert us. He never has, and He never will. He cannot do it. It is not His character [to do so]."[102]

Elder Boyd K. Packer taught that "there is no habit, no addiction, no rebellion, no transgression, no apostasy, no crime exempted from the promise of complete forgiveness."[103] "It is not possible for you to sink lower," Elder Jeffrey R. Holland testified, "than the infinite light of Christ's Atonement shines."[104] This is what Paul meant when he said we were simply incapable of fathoming the "breadth, and length, and depth, and height" of Christ's love.[105]

That is what C. S. Lewis believed: "No amount of falls will really undo us if we keep on picking ourselves up each time. We shall of course be very muddy and tattered children by the time we reach home. But the bathrooms are all ready, the towels put out, the clean clothes in the airing cupboard. The only fatal thing is to lose one's temper and give up."[106] Let us also assume that as no sin is too grave, no moment is too late for repentance. That still leaves the question in many minds, what if the desire to repent never comes into the equation? If a loved one has rejected the gospel under the best of conditions, what basis for hope do we have? If one awakes across the veil with the familiar disposition, hardened in our lifelong habits, why expect repentance then? The theologian Kenneth Kirk provides a compelling answer:

> Three things are true about love. . . . The first is, that it always confers independence upon the object of its love. It gives, compelling no return; it goes on giving, though no love is given in answer. It is the one force in the world which does not bargain. . . . Second, if love endows the *recipient* with formal freedom—with the right to accept or reject at will—it also, and it alone, confers upon the *giver* actual freedom. . . . In love and in love alone can [humankind] actualize the freedom . . . which God has given him. . . . Man becomes free as he learns to love. And finally, love is irresistible . . . and therefore whatever in the end opposes it must in the end give way. . . . The same power which confers freedom on its recipients also evokes from them—not by contract, not by force, but by the invincible suasion of a moral appeal—an answer of love freely given in return.[107]

This was the original capacious vision that early Church Fathers, including Origen, shared with other Christians in those first generations after Christ, that "The Word shall prevail over the entire rational creation, and change every soul into His own perfection; . . . every one, by the mere exercise of his power, will choose what he desires, and obtain what he chooses. For although, in the diseases and wounds of the body, there are some which no medical skill can cure, yet we hold that in the mind there is no evil so strong that it may not be overcome by the Supreme Word of God. For stronger than all the evils in the soul is the Word, and the healing power that dwells in Him; and this healing He applies, according to the will of God, to every man."[108] As one commentator summarizes, "God's infinite love and patience will prevail and will wear down the resistance of even the most rebellious souls."[109]

"Love is irresistible. . . . Whatever in the end opposes it must in the end give way." The gentle-hearted poet Thomas Traherne explained why. "No man can sin that clearly seeth the beauty of God's face, because no man can sin against his own happiness. That is, none can, when he sees it clearly, willingly and wittingly forsake it."[110] Gregory of Nyssa's sister, the early Christian Macrina, spoke in similar terms of our inability permanently to resist Christ's entreaties: "Love is the life of God, and it cannot be otherwise, since perfect beauty is necessarily lovable to those who recognize it; and out of this recognition comes love. The insolence of satiety cannot touch this perfect beauty, nor can satiety ever put a stop to man's power to love what is entirely beautiful; and so the life of God consists in the eternal practice of love; and this life is wholly beautiful, possessed of a loving disposition toward beauty and never receiving any check in the practice of love. And because beauty is boundless, love shall never cease."[111]

For all these reasons, we find plentiful seeds of hope that Christ will truly wipe away all tears. When the sons and daughters of the morning shouted for joy at the Parents' plan, it was certainly a joy tinged with grief at the cost. However, we believe it is unlikely we would have rejoiced at a proposal that would—in the end—permanently disperse families, sever connections, and shut the doors of heaven to multitudes. The power behind Christ's Atonement was the unfathomable and irresistible love of a Savior who "layeth down his own life that he may draw *all* men unto him."[112] Sooner. Or later. We may ask with Enos, "Lord, how is it done?"[113] Or we may simply marvel, along with Julian of Norwich, given the stubbornness and faithlessness of so many. We too may think "it was impossible that every kind of thing should be well." Nonetheless, she wrote in wonder, "I had no other answer . . . from our Lord God except this: What is impossible to you is not impossible to me: I shall preserve my word in everything, and I shall make everything well"[114] because *"a shepherd hath called after you and is still calling after you."*[115]

Epilogue

Where lies your landmark, seamark, or soul's star?
—GERARD MANLEY HOPKINS[1]

Culturally, we in the modern world have lost our collective innocence. The philosopher Charles Taylor designates our era "the Secular Age," meaning a period in which faith has ceased to be a given. We no longer, as the poet Robinson Jeffers lamented, wake up day by day like Homer, "taking the stars and the gods for granted."[2] Belief in God is no longer an inherited assumption, but an effortful decision to be made, one of many options. Some critics have noted that the common substance of almost all novels in the Western tradition is the movement from childhood naiveté to painful disillusionment (the Germans give a particular name to this genre: *Bildungsroman,* or novel of formation). Voltaire's Candide, Mark Twain's Huck Finn, Charles Dickens's Pip, Jane Austen's Catherine, and a thousand other protagonists learn that life is suffering. These writers capture the unmistakable truth: None of us reaches adulthood unscathed. To be grown-up means to be wary, cautious. To be educated often means in practice to be critical, cynical, and suspicious. Freud taught us to look for unconscious motives behind all conscious actions; Marx argued that economic self-interest motivates us all; Nietzsche convinced multitudes that religion itself is a con game perpetrated on the unsuspecting; post-modernists alert us to hidden power dynamics that exploit and oppress; and Richard Dawkins argues that our very genes conspire to perpetuate themselves independent of our conscious volition. Media manipulates us, advertisers seduce us, and everyone digs a pit for the neighbor. If we are not unhinged by paranoia, we emerge from the maelstrom of these hermeneutics of suspicion with a jaundiced eye and a bruised spirit.

Life in the Church adds its own varieties of hammer blows to our innocence. We learn that leaders are fallible, scriptures err, and Church commitments can feel more of a burden than a blessing. Tithing does not always preserve us from penury, the Word of Wisdom does not guarantee freedom from disease, and our ardent prayers may find neither answer nor response. Notwithstanding our faithful efforts—including temple attendance and family home evenings—marriages fail, families fracture, and children choose other paths. The choice to believe weighs upon us heavily, and for many of us, faith—and the burdens of belief—we find are at last too heavy to carry. "Because we are not divine," notes the author Mark Helprin, "we must jettison the many burdens we cannot bear."[3] Being mortal, we are tempted to relinquish our faith to the swirling currents of doubt, fear, skepticism, and cynicism that engulf our culture.

How can our faith thrive, or even survive, in times such as these? We both find plentiful motives to bind our hearts to the restored gospel. Its theology, its community, its gospel fruits all register powerfully with us. Within the broad expanse of religious systems, we find that Restoration teachings provide the most compelling account of our spirit's origins and destiny, life's purpose, and God's nature. We feel the pull of premortal realms and resonate with the truth that life is educative, purposeful, and designed for our growth. We adore a God who does not recoil in jealous insecurity because "man is become as one of us,"[4] but invites us to share in the divine nature and has the wisdom and power to bring the entire human family home. We have experienced a community of true belonging, and we sense

EPILOGUE

the outlines of Zion in flawed but caring wards and a familiar spirit wherever and whenever we have encountered Saints. Joseph made friendship and kinship the warp and woof of the gospel, weaving their fibers through the structures of a church where all are invited to minister to one another; then he extended the domain of these associations into the eternities.

Finally, we have tasted the fruits of the Restoration in the peace, joy, and love we have found as we labor to live its teachings. Its template has strengthened our family bonds and prodded us to live more selflessly and purposefully. The rich scriptural canon of Mormonism and the prophetic voice have been invaluable resources for helping us negotiate the perils of life in this world.

The apostle Paul likewise praised the gifts of the gospel, but realized the imperfect hold that they can have on discipleship. "Whether there be prophecies, they shall fail; whether there be tongues, they shall cease; whether there be knowledge, it shall vanish away," he acknowledged.[5] We recognize, in the lives of many friends and loved ones, that the abstractions of theology can lose their compelling appeal; communities can let us down and frustrate more than inspire; and our lives are not always marked by the peace, the joy, and the love that we had hoped to find here. Only charity, said Paul, never falters. Only "the rock of our Redeemer, who is Christ," taught Helaman, is a sure foundation that never fails.[6]

In the catacombs of St. Priscilla, outside Rome, where early generations of Christians worshipped and where they buried their dead, are the earliest known examples of Christian art. While visiting there recently we passed one remarkable fresco. On the ancient wall was a rendering of the scene prophetically seen and described by the prophet Nephi. In colors now faded but still perceptible, a virgin cradles a baby in her arms. We both stopped short as we noticed that they are sheltered beneath the fruit-laden boughs of a magnificent tree. "The Tree of Life," confirmed the tour guide leading the way.

In Nephi's messianic vision, following in his father's prophetic footsteps, he beheld a tree of surpassing beauty. "And the whiteness thereof did exceed the whiteness of the driven snow."[7] The tree faded from his sight, to be replaced by "a virgin, most beautiful and fair above all other virgins."[8] Moments later, Nephi saw this same virgin holding a child, and then the Spirit spoke to him: "Behold the Lamb of God, yea, even the Son of the Eternal Father! Knowest thou the meaning of the tree which thy father saw? And I answered him, saying: Yea, it is the love of God, which sheddeth itself abroad in the hearts of the children of men; wherefore, it is the most desirable above all things."[9]

Paul and Helaman were teaching the same thing. Only charity never fails us. Only Jesus Christ the Healer is a sure foundation. Because they are the same. The most perfect form of love the universe has ever known is fully realized in the Christ of the Restoration. Encountering that reality is the sole means of anchoring our faith in the Restoration on unassailable foundations, moving us from fragile faith to the durable discipleship of love. Only truth that is hard won, dearly bought, and firmly grasped can nourish and sustain us through the crucible of life, of doubt, of loss. Like the philosopher's stone of legend, the foundation we build in Christ can transmute the earthy elements of our poor selves into celestial material fit for glory if that foundation be laid in a correct understanding. We believe this is true for one simple reason. In that dramatic colloquy in the Tower with his daughter Meg, who complains, "Haven't you done as much as God can reasonably want?," Robert Bolt's Thomas More explains, "Well finally, it isn't a matter of reason. Finally, it's a matter of love."[10] Even to begin to know our Heavenly Parents and their Christ, through the prism of the restored gospel that we have tried to illuminate, is inevitably and irresistibly to love them with a love that is healing, transformative, and redemptive.

In one of the nineteenth century's most charming poems on the bliss of young passion, the poet John Keats contemplates his own imminent death. Imagining separation from his beloved, he weeps that

EPILOGUE

I shall never look upon thee more,
Never have relish in the faery power
Of unreflecting love.[11]

Unreflecting love is indeed a charming phase, but like all infatuations, it is more glitter than gold, more delightful than durable. Real love—like genuine friendship and companionate marriage—is deeply reflective and self-aware. We have tried to convey something of the depths of our understanding of, appreciation for, and faith in the Christ of the Restoration. In coming to know this Christ, we feel to echo words written centuries before the Restoration blessed the world: "I do not love thee for the promised heaven. I do not worship thee from fear of hell."[12] We love him because he first loved us. With a depth and beauty beyond all imagining.

NOTES

SETTING THE STAGE

1. 1 Nephi 13:28.
2. Justin, "How the Word Has Been in All Men," in *The Writings of Justin Martyr and Athenagoras*, eds. Marcus Dods, George Reith, and B. P. Pratten (Edinburgh: T. & T. Clark, 1867), 83.
3. Tertullian, *The Writings of Quintus Sept. Flor. Tertullianus*, vol. 2, trans. Peter Holmes (Edinburgh: T. & T. Clark, 1884), 504, 9, 173.
4. Augustine, *The Confessions of S. Augustine*, ed. Rev. E. B. Pusey, D.D. (Oxford: John Henry Parker, 1853), 1.
5. Sabapathy Kulandran, *Grace in Christianity and Hinduism: A Comparative Study* (Cambridge: James Clarke & Co., 2004), 77.
6. Ignatius, *The Epistle of S. Ignatius*, in *The Apostolic Fathers*, ed. and trans. J.B. Lightfoot (London: Macmillan and Company, 1898), 142.
7. Charles H. Hoole, ed., *The Apostolic Fathers: The Epistles of S. Clement, S. Ignatius, S. Barnabas, S. Polycarp, together with the Martyrdom of S. Ignatius and S. Polycarp* (London: Rivingtons, 1872), l.
8. Polycarp, *Martyrdom of Polycarp*, in *The Epistles of Ignatius and Polycarp*, trans. W. K. Clementson (Brighton: Creasy and Baker, 1827), 100.
9. Irenaeus, *The Writings of Irenaeus*, vol. 2, trans. Rev. Alexander Roberts, D.D., and Rev. W. H. Rambaut, A.B. (Edinburgh: T. & T. Clark, 1869), 159.
10. Irenaeus, *Against Heresies* V, in *The Early Christian Fathers*, ed. and trans. Henry Bettenson (Oxford: Oxford University Press, 1969), 77.
11. Saint Clement, *The Writings of Clement of Alexandria*, vol. 2, trans. Rev. William Wilson, M.A. (Edinburgh: T. & T. Clark, 1869), 487.
12. Saint Clement, *The Writings of Clement of Alexandria*, vol. 1, trans. Rev. William Wilson, M.A. (Edinburgh: T. & T. Clark, 1867), 24.
13. Origen, *Man*, in *Early Christian Fathers*, 274.
14. Morwenna Ludlow, *Universal Salvation* (Oxford: Oxford University Press, 2000), 61.
15. Gregory Nazianzus, *On the Words of the Gospel*, in *A Select Library of Nicene and Post-Nicene Fathers of the Christian Church*, 2nd series vol. 7, eds. and trans. Henry Wace, D.D., and Philip Schaff, D.D., L.L.D. (New York: The Christian Literature Company, 1894), 339.

NOTES

16. Robert Payne, *The Fathers of the Eastern Church* (New York: Dorset Press, 1989), 146.
17. Martin Luther, *Faith and Freedom: An Invitation to the Writings of Martin Luther*, eds. John F. Thornton and Susan B. Varenne (New York: Vintage Books, 2002), 95.
18. John Calvin, *Isaiah*, eds. Alister McGrath and J. I. Packer (Wheaton, IL: Crossway Books, 2000).
19. Julian of Norwich, *Sixteen Revelations of Divine Love* (London: S. Clarke, 1843), 84; *Showings*, trans. Edmund Colledge, O.S.A., and James Walsh, S.J. (Mahwah, NJ: Paulist Press, 1978), 181.
20. Edward Beecher, *The Concord of Ages* (New York: Derby & Jackson, 1860), 156.
21. Nikolai A. Berdyaev, "The Truth of Orthodoxy," http://www.chebucto.ns.ca/Philosophy/Sui-Generis/Berdyaev/essays/orthodox.htm, 4 (originally published in *Vestnik of the Russian West European Patriarchal Exarchate* [Paris, 1952]).

INTRODUCTION

1. Tertullian, *De Carne Christi* 4, in *The Early Christian Fathers*, ed. and trans. Henry Bettenson (Oxford: Oxford University Press, 1956), 126.
2. D&C 20:59; 49:8.
3. D&C 90:15; see also 91:1.
4. Joseph Smith, *The Words of Joseph Smith*, eds. Andrew F. Ehat and Lyndon W. Cook (Orem, UT: Grandin Book Company, 1991), 229.
5. "Presbyterians any truth, embrace that. Baptist. Methodist &c. get all the good in the world, come out a pure Mormon." Smith, *Words*, 234.
6. Matthew 16:15; emphasis added.
7. It is important to note that in both Genesis 5:2 and Moses 6:9 the term *Adam* is familial: "and [he] called their name Adam" in the same way that the term *God* can incorporate both a male and female deity.
8. Moses 6:5–6.
9. 3 Nephi 11:3.
10. 3 Nephi 17:15, 17.
11. See, in this regard, *The Joseph Smith Papers: Revelations and Translations, Manuscript Revelation Books*, ed. Robin Scott Jensen, Robert J. Woodford, and Steven C. Harper (Salt Lake City: Church Historian's Press, 2009), which reproduces the oldest existing copies of Joseph's revelations, indicating the editorial hand of several colleagues.
12. Joseph Smith to William W. Phelps, November 27, 1832, in *Personal Writings of Joseph Smith*, comp. Dean C. Jessee, rev. ed. (Salt Lake City: Deseret Book, 2002), 287.
13. D&C 1:24; emphasis added.
14. *The Complete Discourses of Brigham Young*, ed. Richard S. Van Wagoner (Salt Lake City: Smith-Petit Foundation, 2009), 4:2033.
15. 1 Nephi 13:28.
16. Smith, *Words*, 211.
17. Ibid., 319.
18. Joseph Smith—History 1:19.
19. Dieter F. Uchtdorf, "He Will Place You on His Shoulders and Carry You Home," *Ensign*, May 2016, 101–4.

NOTES

20. Edward Beecher, *The Concord of Ages* (New York: Derby & Jackson, 1860), 156.
21. *Lectures on Faith* (Salt Lake City: Deseret Book, 1985), 38.
22. 2 Corinthians 5:17.

PART 1: THE GOSPEL BEFORE THE RESTORATION

1. "The Religion of the Ancients," *Times and Seasons* 4.9 (15 March 1843): 137.
2. Not the Prophet, S.T.P., "To the Editor," *Times and Seasons* 5.8 (15 April 1844): 503.

CHAPTER 1: COVENANT

1. *The Song of the Pearl*, trans. Han J. W. Drijvers, Robert M. Grant, Bentley Layton, and Willis Barnstone. In Barnstone and Marvin Meyer, eds., *The Gnostic Bible* (Boston: Shambhala, 2003), 388.
2. M. Russell Ballard, *When Thou Art Converted: Continuing Our Search for Happiness* (Salt Lake City: Deseret Book, 2001), 62.
3. See the section "Coframer of the Plan of Salvation" in David Paulsen and Martin Pulido, "A Mother There: A Survey of Historical Teachings about Mother in Heaven," *BYU Studies* 50:1 (2011): 80–82.
4. Stan Larson, "The King Follett Discourse: A Newly Amalgamated Text," *BYU Studies* 18.2 (Winter 1978): 204.
5. *Journal of Discourses*, 26 vols., reported by G. D. Watt et al. Liverpool: F.D. and S. W. Richards, et al., 1851–1886 (reprint Salt Lake City: n.p., 1974), 19:266.
6. https://www.lds.org/topics/mother-in-heaven?lang=eng&old=true.
7. D&C 49:16–17.
8. "Covenant," *Encyclopedia Judaica* (Jerusalem: Keter Publishing House, 1996), 5:1021.
9. Howard Schwartz, *The Tree of Souls: The Mythology of Judaism* (Oxford: Oxford University Press, 2004), 161.
10. *Midrash Tanhuma Pekude* III.11, in Avrohom Davis, trans., *The Metsudah Midrash Tanchuma: Shemos II* (New York: Judaica Press, 2004), vol. 2, part 2:402.
11. Mensasseh ben Israel, *De Creatione Problemata XXX*, cited in Johannes van den Berg, "Menasseh ben Israel, Henry More, and Johannes Hoornbeeck on the Pre-Existence of the Soul," *Religious Currents and Cross-Currents: Essays on Early Modern Protestantism*, eds. Jan de Bruijn, Pieter Holtrop, and Ernestine van der Wall (Leiden: Brill, 1999), 66.
12. H. Wheeler Robinson, "The Council of Yahweh," *Journal of Theological Studies* 45.179/180 (1944): 151.
13. Jon D. Levenson, *Sinai and Zion: An Entry into the Jewish Bible* (New York: HarperOne, 1985), 41.
14. Ibid.
15. Origen, *De Principiis* I.vi.3, in *The Ante-Nicene Fathers*, ed. Alexander Roberts and James Donaldson (Grand Rapids, MI: Eerdmans, 1977), 4:261.
16. *Times and Seasons* 3.10 (15 March 1842): 720; Abraham 3:24, 26.
17. Joseph Smith, *The Words of Joseph Smith*, eds. Andrew F. Ehat and Lyndon W. Cook (Orem, UT: Grandin Book Company, 1991), 253.
18. Robert Frost, "Trial by Existence," *A Boy's Will* (New York: Henry Holt, 1915), 41.

NOTES

19. *The Song of the Pearl*, in Barnstone and Meyer, eds., *Gnostic Bible*, 388–89.
20. Moses 5:11.
21. Genesis 3:22.
22. 2 Nephi 2:25; John Milton, *Paradise Lost* I.ii.3–4 (New York: Penguin, 2000), 3.
23. Roger E. Olson, *The Story of Christian Theology* (Downers Grove, IL: InterVarsity Press, 1999), 77.

Chapter 2: God

1. Daniel Bourguet, *The Tenderness of God* (Eugene, OR: Wipf and Stock, 2016), 6.
2. Justin Martyr, *Dialogue with Trypho* LVI, in *The Ante-Nicene Fathers*, ed. Alexander Roberts and James Donaldson (Grand Rapids, MI: Eerdmans, 1977), 1:223.
3. Denis Minns, *Irenaeus* (London: T. & T. Clark, 2010), 58.
4. Celsus, *On the True Doctrine*, cited in Roger E. Olson, *The Story of Christian Theology* (Downers Grove, IL: InterVarsity Press, 1999), 34.
5. J. N. D. Kelly, *Early Christian Doctrines* (San Francisco: HarperSan Francisco, 1978), 88.
6. Origen, *Contra Celsum* viii. 12, in *The Early Christian Fathers*, ed. and trans. Henry Bettenson (Oxford: Oxford University Press, 1956), 243.
7. Olson, *Story of Christian Theology*, 35.
8. Ibid., 52.
9. Marcellino D'Ambrosio, *Who Were the Church Fathers* (London: SPCK, 2015), 15.
10. Romans 8:15.
11. John 20:17.
12. Clement of Alexandria, *Stromata* V.xi, in *Ante-Nicene Fathers*, 2:461.
13. John Meyendorff, *Byzantine Theology: Historical Trends and Doctrinal Themes* (New York: Fordham University Press, 1999), 12.
14. See Tertullian, *Apology* xvii, in *Ante-Nicene Fathers*, 3:31–32.
15. Minns, *Irenaeus*, 32.
16. Nikolai Berdyaev, *Freedom and The Spirit* (London: Geoffrey Bles, 1935), 189.
17. Marie Magdalene Davy, *Nicolas Berdyaev: Man of the Eighth Day* (London: Geoffrey Bles, 1967), 63.
18. Minns, *Irenaeus*, 42.
19. Irenaeus, *Against Heresies* II.xiii.3, in *Ante-Nicene Fathers*, 1:374.
20. Irenaeus, *Against Heresies* IV.xx.7, in *Ante-Nicene Fathers*, 1:489.
21. Tertullian, *Treatise on the Soul* XXIV, in *Ante-Nicene Fathers*, 3:203.
22. John Sanders, *The God Who Risks* (Downers Grove, IL: InterVarsity Press, 2007), 41.
23. Origen, *Hom. in Ezechielem* vi.6, in *Early Christian Fathers*, 186–87.
24. Richard Bauckham, "'Only the Suffering God Can Help': Divine Passibility in Modern Theology," *Themelios* 9.3 (April 1984): 6.
25. See Marcel Sarot, *God, Passibility, and Corporeality* (Kampen, Netherlands: Pharos, 1992), 1–2.
26. Jaroslav Pelikan and Valerie Hotchkiss, *Creeds and Confessions of Faith in the Christian Tradition* (New Haven, CT: Yale University Press, 2003), 2:626.
27. Davy, *Nicolas Berdyaev: Man of the Eighth Day*, 62–63.
28. John 14:9.
29. Augustine, *Sermon* 88.4; Ambrose, *Sermon Against Auxentius* 32; Hilary of

NOTES

Poitiers, *On the Trinity* 7:40. All found in *Ancient Christian Commentary on Scripture: John 11–21*, ed. Joel C. Elowsky (Downers Grove, IL: InterVarsity Press, 2007), New Testament IVb:131–32.
30. Theodore of Mopsuestia, *Commentary on John* 6.14.10, in *Ancient Christian Commentary*, IVb:132.
31. John Milton, *Paradise Lost* III. ii.56–98 (New York: Penguin, 2000), 54–55.
32. Augustine, *The Essential Augustine*, ed. Vernon J. Bourke (Indianapolis: Hackett, 1974), 61.
33. Olson, *Story of Christian Theology*, 255–56.
34. T. Kermit Scott, *Augustine: His Thought in Context* (Mahwah, New Jersey: Paulist, 1995), 153. Cited in Olson, *Story of Christian Theology*, 256.
35. Martin Luther, *The Bondage of the Will*, ed. Henry Cole (Lexington, KY: Feather Trail Press, 2009), 14.
36. Ibid., 18.
37. John Calvin, *Institutes* III.xxiii.6, in *Institutes of the Christian Religion*, trans. Henry Beveridge (Peabody, MA: Hendrickson, 2008), 629.
38. *The Confession of Faith* (Glasgow: Bell and Bain, 1985), 26.
39. Ibid., 196.
40. Luther, *Bondage*, 33.
41. See Moses 7.
42. Arthur Masson, ed., *A Collection of English Prose and Verse for the Use of Schools*, seventh ed. (Edinburgh: 1773), 196.
43. *The Joseph Smith Papers: Histories, Volume 1*, ed. Karen Lynn Davidson, David J. Whittaker, Mark Ashurst-McGee, and Richard L. Jensen (Salt Lake City: Church Historian's Press, 2012), 12.
44. See James 1:5.

Chapter 3: The Fall

1. Irenaeus, *Against Heresies* III.xxiii.3, in *The Ante-Nicene Fathers*, ed. Alexander Roberts and James Donaldson (Grand Rapids, MI: Eerdmans, 1977), 1:456.
2. Moses 6:54.
3. Philo of Alexandria, *Quaestiones et Solutiones in Genesin* [*Questions and Answers on Genesis*] IV (74), in *The Contemplative Life, The Giants, and Selections*, ed. and trans. David Winston (Mahwah, NJ: Paulist, 1981), 119.
4. 1 Corinthians 15:22; Romans 5:12. For a discussion of how Romans 5:12 was misinterpreted as a foundation for original sin through the mistranslation of the fourth century Ambrosiaster, see Terryl Givens, *Wrestling the Angel* (New York: Oxford University Press, 2014), 177ff.
5. See Eusebius, *History of the Church* 5:20:5–7, quoted in Anthony Zimmerman, *Evolution and the Sin in Eden* (Lanham, MD: University Press of America, 1998), 148–49.
6. Irenaeus, *Against Heresies* III.xxxiii.6, in *Ante-Nicene Fathers*, 1:457.
7. Irenaeus, *Against Heresies*, IV.xxxix.1–2, in *Ante-Nicene Fathers*, 1:522.
8. Origen, *Homilies on Numbers* XXVII.xi, in Antonia Tripolitis, *Doctrine of the Soul in the Thought of Plotinus and Origen* (Roslyn Heights, NY: Libra, 1977), 126; and *De Principiis* II.xi.6–7, paraphrased in Tripolitis, *Doctrine of the Soul*, 133.
9. Irenaeus, *Against Heresies* IV.xxxvii.7, in *Ante-Nicene Fathers*, 1:520–21.
10. Zimmerman, *Evolution*, 160.

NOTES

11. Ibid., 157.
12. Ibid.
13. Gregory of Nyssa, *De beatitudinibus* 6, in Robert Payne, *The Fathers of the Eastern Church* (New York: Dorset, 1989), xv.
14. Martin Luther, *The Bondage of the Will*, ed. Henry Cole (Lexington, KY: Feather Trail, 2009), 22.
15. Payne, *Fathers of the Eastern Church*, xiv; Gregory of Nyssa, *De beatitudinibus* 6, and Gregory Palamas, *De hominis Opificio* IV, 136, both in Payne, xiv–xv.
16. Job 19:26; Luke 24:39.
17. Tertullian, *On the Resurrection of the Flesh*, in *Ante-Nicene Fathers*, 3:551.
18. Ibid.
19. Clement of Alexandria, *The Instructor* I.xiii, in *Ante-Nicene Fathers*, 2:235.
20. Moses 6:59, 1851 edition.
21. Zimmerman (*Evolution*, 160) is citing Denis Minns, *Irenaeus* (London: T. & T. Clark, 2010), 61. The reference to Irenaeus is *Against Heresies* III.xx.2; Zimmerman, *Evolution*, 153.
22. Zimmerman, *Evolution*, 160.
23. Julian of Norwich, *Showing* XIV, chap. 51 in *Showings*, trans. Edmund Colledge and James Walsh (Mahwah, NJ: Paulist Press, 1978), 267–70.
24. Thomas Traherne, "Wonder," in *Selected Writings*, ed. Dick Davis (Manchester: Fyfield, 1980), 20.
25. Nikolai Berdyaev, quoted in Marie Magdalene Davy, *Nicolas Berdyaev: Man of the Eighth Day* (London: Geoffrey Bles, 1967), 86–87.
26. John A. Widtsoe, *Evidences and Reconciliations* (Salt Lake City: Bookcraft, 1947), 2:78.
27. We use the term *prophets* not in the sense of an office or holder of priesthood keys, but in John's sense of an inspired man or woman bearing "testimony of Jesus" (Revelation 19:10).

Chapter 4: Agency

1. Irenaeus, *Against Heresies* IV.xxxvii.4, in *The Ante-Nicene Fathers*, ed. Alexander Roberts and James Donaldson (Grand Rapids, MI: Eerdmans, 1977), 1:519.
2. Chrysostom, *De proditione Judaeorum* homily 1, cited in Calvin, *Institutes* II.ii.4, in John Calvin, *Institutes of the Christian Religion*, trans. Henry Beveridge (Peabody, MA: Hendrickson, 2008), 159.
3. See John 8:32.
4. *Diognetus*, 7:4, cited in Marcellino D'Ambrosio, *Who Were the Church Fathers* (London: SPCK, 2015), 44.
5. Augustine, *Reconsiderations* 1.9, in *On Free Choice of the Will*, trans. Thomas Williams (Indianapolis: Hackett, 1993), 127, 125.
6. The expression was *"sed vicit Dei gratia,"* in Augustine, *Retractions* II.27, trans. Mary Inez Bogan (Washington: Catholic University of America Press, 1968), 12; Robert J. O'Connell, *Images of Conversion in St. Augustine's Confessions* (New York: Fordham University Press, 1996), 305.
7. John Meyendorff, *Byzantine Theology: Historical Trends and Doctrinal Themes* (New York: Fordham University Press, 1999), 143.
8. Calvin, *Institutes* II.ii.4, in Calvin, *Institutes of the Christian Religion*, 160; "All

NOTES

ancient theologians, with the exception of Augustine" were "confused" on the subject, he wrote.

9. Calvin, *Institutes* III.xxiii.14, in ibid., 634.
10. Martin Luther, *The Bondage of the Will*, ed. Henry Cole (Lexington, KY: Feather Trail, 2009), 30–32.
11. Ibid., 18.
12. Ibid., 29.
13. He refutes the Catholics who argue that "the wicked perish only by the permission, but not by the will, of God." See Calvin, *Institutes* III.xxiii.8, in Calvin, *Institutes of the Christian Religion*, 630.
14. Ibid.
15. Calvin, *Institutes* III.xxiii.7, in ibid., 629.
16. *Westminster Confession III*, in Jaroslav Pelikan and Valerie Hotchkiss, *Creeds and Confessions of Faith in the Christian Tradition* (New Haven, CT: Yale University Press, 2003), 2:610.
17. Joseph Smith, *The Words of Joseph Smith*, eds. Andrew F. Ehat and Lyndon W. Cook (Orem, UT: Grandin Book Company, 1991), 33.
18. 2 Nephi 2:2.
19. Ecclesiastes 9:11.
20. *Westminster Confession III*, in Pelikan and Hotchkiss, *Creeds and Confessions*, 2:610.
21. Paul Ricoeur, "On Consolation," in Alasdair MacIntyre and Paul Ricoeur, *The Religious Significance of Atheism* (New York: Columbia University Press, 1969), 88.
22. Rachael Givens, "Mormonism and the Dilemma of Tragedy," *Patheos*, http://www.patheos.com/blogs/peculiarpeople/2012/05/mormonism-and-the-dilemma-of-tragedy/, cited in Terryl Givens and Fiona Givens, *The God Who Weeps* (Salt Lake City: Deseret Book, 2012), 33.
23. C. S. Lewis, *Perelandra* (New York: Scribner, 1996), 129.

Chapter 5: Sin

1. Tertullian, *On the Soul* XLI, in *The Ante-Nicene Fathers*, ed. Alexander Roberts and James Donaldson (Grand Rapids, MI: Eerdmans, 1977), 3:220.
2. George Gordon, Lord Byron, "Prometheus," lines 47–48.
3. 1 Corinthians 15:22.
4. 2 Nephi 9:10–11.
5. Irenaeus, *Against Heresies* IV.xxxviii.4, in *The Early Christian Fathers*, ed. and trans. Henry Bettenson (Oxford: Oxford University Press, 1969), 69.
6. John Meyendorff, *Byzantine Theology: Historical Trends and Doctrinal Themes* (New York: Fordham University Press, 1999), 143, 145.
7. Julian of Norwich, *Showing* XIII, chap. 27 in *Showings*, trans. Edmund Colledge and James Walsh (Mahwah, NJ: Paulist Press, 1978), 224–25.
8. Meister Eckhart, "Talks of Instruction," in *Meister Eckhart*, trans. Raymond B. Blakney (New York: Harper and Row, 1941), 12.
9. Meyendorff, *Byzantine Theology*, 143.
10. Elaine Pagels, *Adam, Eve, and the Serpent* (New York: Vintage, 1989), 99.
11. J. A. Quenstedt, *Theologia didactico-polemica* (Wittenberg, 1691), 134 ff. Cited in Norman P. Williams, *The Ideas of the Fall and Original Sin* (London: Longmans, Green, 1929), 429.

NOTES

12. Augustine, "On Psalm 18," *The Essential Augustine*, ed. Vernon J. Bourke (Indianapolis: Hackett, 1974), 188–89.
13. "Formula of Concord: Epitome" [8] 3, in Jaroslav Pelikan and Valerie Hotchkiss, *Creeds and Confessions of Faith in the Christian Tradition* (New Haven, CT: Yale University Press, 2003), 2:170.
14. "Formula of Concord," in Pelikan and Hotchkiss, *Creeds and Confessions* [16] 6, 2:171.
15. "Thirty-Nine Articles of the Church of England" IX, XIII, in Pelikan and Hotchkiss, *Creeds and Confessions*, 2:531.
16. John Calvin, *Institutes* II.ii.1, in *Institutes of the Christian Religion*, trans. Henry Beveridge (Peabody, MA: Hendrickson, 2008), 157.
17. R. K. Johnston, "Imputation," *Evangelical Dictionary of Theology*, ed. Walter A. Elwell (Grand Rapids, MI: Baker Academic, 2001), 600.
18. Calvin, *Institutes* III.xiv.12–13, in *Institutes of the Christian Religion*, 510.
19. Alister E. McGrath, "Justification," *Oxford Encyclopedia of the Reformation*, ed. Hans J. Hillerbrand (New York: Oxford University Press, 1996), 2:362–63.
20. Neal A. Maxwell, "Notwithstanding My Weakness," *Ensign*, November 1976, 14.
21. Irenaeus, *Against Heresies* V.xvi.1, in *Ante-Nicene Fathers*, 1:544.
22. John Milton, *Paradise Lost* IX.ii.335–41 (New York: Penguin, 2000), 335.
23. Moses 6:55.

PART 2: ALL THINGS MADE NEW

1. Joseph Smith, in *Elders Journal* (July 1838): 44.

CHAPTER 6: THE SELFLESS CHRIST

1. The Universal Declaration of Human Rights was produced by the United Nations in 1948. It can be found at http://www.un.org/en/universal-declaration-human-rights/index.html.
2. Origen, *Against Celsus* IV.vii, in *The Ante-Nicene Fathers*, ed. Alexander Roberts and James Donaldson (Grand Rapids, MI: Eerdmans, 1977), 4:500.
3. Irenaeus, *Against Heresies*, IV.xxxvii.4, in *The Early Christian Fathers*, ed. and trans. Henry Bettenson (Oxford: Oxford University Press, 1969), 69.
4. Tertullian, *Apology* XVII, in *Ante-Nicene Fathers*, 3:31.
5. Thomas Watson, "Man's Chief End Is to Glorify God," in *A Body of Practical Divinity* (Philadelphia, PA: T. Wardle, 1833), 8.
6. Roger E. Olson, *The Story of Christian Theology* (Downers Grove, IL: InterVarsity Press, 1999), 506.
7. *The Catechism of Christian Doctrine, Prepared and Enjoined by Order of the Third Council of Baltimore* became the standard catechism in American Catholic schools (Philadelphia, PA: Cunningham and Son, 1885).
8. http://rickwarren.org/devotional/english/you-were-made-for-god-s-glory.
9. John Piper, *The Pleasures of God* (Colorado Springs: Multnomah Books, 2012), 29, 192.
10. Joseph Smith, *The Words of Joseph Smith*, eds. Andrew F. Ehat and Lyndon W. Cook (Orem, UT: Grandin Book Company, 1991), 247.
11. *The Complete Discourses of Brigham Young*, ed. Richard S. Van Wagoner (Salt Lake City: Smith-Petit Foundation, 2009), 1:559.

NOTES

12. 2 Nephi 2:25.
13. Plato, *Timaeus* 29e, trans. Donald J. Zeyl, Alexander Nehamas, and Paul Woodruff, in *Plato: Complete Works*, ed. John M. Cooper (Indianapolis: Hackett, 1997), 1236.
14. Moses 1:39.
15. Theodore M. Burton, "A Marriage to Last through Eternity," *Ensign*, June 1987, 14.
16. 2 Nephi 26:24.

Chapter 7: The Adoptive Christ

1. *The Joseph Smith Papers: Documents, Volume 7*, ed. Matthew C. Godfrey, Spencer W. McBride, Alex D. Smith, and Christopher James Blythe (Salt Lake City: Church Historian's Press, forthcoming).
2. This replacement is alluded to by Paul in Galatians, writing "the law . . . was added because of transgressions" (3:19). Joseph clarifies that this replacement took place with Moses, and not Adam, in his new translation of Exodus 34:1, wherein he describes God delivering a different set of tablets after the first are destroyed.
3. John 17:22, 24.
4. Cited in James E. Talmage, *The Articles of Faith* (Salt Lake City: Deseret News, 1968), 467–68.
5. Walter Kasper, *Mercy: The Essence of the Gospel and the Key to Christian Life*, trans. William Madges (New York: Paulist Press, 2013), 44–45.
6. Roger E. Olson, *The Story of Christian Theology* (Downers Grove, IL: InterVarsity Press, 1999), 77.
7. Ignatius, *To the Ephesians*, 20, in Olson, *Story of Christian Theology*, 48.
8. Moses 6:54; Abraham 3:26.
9. *Lectures on Faith* (Salt Lake City: Deseret Book, 1985), 75–76.
10. D&C 13:1; 84:64; Articles of Faith 1:4.
11. 2 Nephi 31:17.
12. Theodoret of Cyrus, *Haeret. fabul. Compendium* 5.18, in John Meyendorff, *Byzantine Theology: Historical Trends and Doctrinal Themes* (New York: Fordham University Press, 1999), 145–46.
13. *The Words of Joseph Smith*, eds. Andrew F. Ehat and Lyndon W. Cook (Orem, UT: Grandin Book Company, 1991), 256. Some Church Fathers and Reformers saw baptism this way, but cleansing from original sin came to dominate the ordinance. Calvin called baptism "the symbol of adoption," and Augustine wrote that "We are adopted into the kingdom of God . . . as his creatures and offspring" (John Calvin, *Institutes* IV.xvi.4, in *Institutes of the Christian Religion*, trans. Henry Beveridge [Peabody, MA: Hendrickson, 2008], 874; Augustine, *Sermon on the Mount* 23.78, in *Ancient Christian Commentary on Scripture, Romans* [Downers Grove, IL: InterVarsity Press, 2005], NT VI:212). However, baptism became almost universally construed as rescue from the effects of original sin.
14. B. H. Roberts, *The Mormon Doctrine of Deity* (Salt Lake City: Deseret News, 1903), 165.
15. Moses 7:33.
16. See Mosiah 18.
17. 2 Nephi 31:13.

NOTES

18. Mosiah 18:10.
19. George Q. Cannon, "Editorial Thoughts," *Juvenile Instructor* 29.15 (1 August 1894): 466–67.
20. "The Father and the Son: A Doctrinal Exposition of the First Presidency and the Twelve," June 30, 1916. In James R. Clark, ed., *Messages of the First Presidency* (Salt Lake City: Bookcraft, 1971), 5:26–34.
21. D&C 20:77.
22. Olson, *Story of Christian Theology*, 48.
23. See Marcellino D'Ambrosio, *Who Were the Church Fathers* (London: SPCK, 2015), 14.
24. D&C 22:1; emphasis added.
25. See Erik Peterson, *Pour une théologie du vêtement*, trans. M.-J. Congar (Lyon: Edition de l'Abeille, 1943), 6–13. Cited in Stephen D. Ricks, "The Garment of Adam," in *Temples of the Ancient World*, ed. Donald W. Parry (Salt Lake City: Deseret Book, 1994), 708.
26. Genesis 3:22; Moses 4:28.
27. Genesis 5:1–2; Moses 2:27.
28. Moses 5:6.
29. Carlos E. Asay, "The Temple Garment: 'An Outward Expression of an Inward Commitment,'" *Ensign*, August 1997, 21.
30. Theodoret of Cyrus, *Haeret. fabul. Compendium* 5.18, in Meyendorff, *Byzantine Theology*, 146.
31. Genesis 3:20.
32. Moses 5:11.
33. Smith, *Words*, 33.

Chapter 8: The Atoning Christ

1. John Milton, *Paradise Lost* VIII l.334 (New York: Penguin, 2000), 175.
2. John Stuart Mill, *On Liberty*, 2nd ed. (Boston: Ticknor and Fields, 1863), 28.
3. 1 Corinthians 13:12.
4. Message to priests delivered on Holy Thursday, 1998; in Anthony Zimmerman, *Evolution and the Sin in Eden* (New York: University Press of America, 1998), 165.
5. Brigham H. Roberts, *The Truth, the Way, the Life*, ed. John Welch (Provo, UT: BYU Studies, 1994), 405.
6. 2 Nephi 2:5, 27.
7. D&C 19:4–17.
8. 2 Nephi 2:11.
9. "By proving contrarieties truth is made manifest," Joseph Smith to Israel Daniel Rupp, June 5, 1824; Manuscript History of the Church, F-1, 70 (in Church History Library).
10. See Terryl Givens, *Wrestling the Angel* (New York: Oxford University Press, 2014), 312ff.
11. The closest preceding atonement theory may be the governmental theory of Hugo Grotius and later Jonathan Mayhew, who believed, in Brooks Holifield's phrase, that "having promulgated a moral law, God could not permit its subversion without allowing the destruction of the moral order itself" (Holifield, *Theology in America* [New Haven, CT: Yale University Press, 2003], 133).

NOTES

12. William Shakespeare, Sonnet 116, *Shakespeare's Sonnets,* ed. Barbara A. Mowat and Paul Werstine (New York: Washington Square Press, 2004), 239.
13. Genesis 15:12.
14. Joseph Smith—History 1:15.
15. John Meyendorff, *Byzantine Theology: Historical Trends and Doctrinal Themes* (New York: Fordham University Press, 1999), 201.
16. Leviticus 17:11.
17. Moses 4:6, 1 Peter 1:4.
18. Jeffrey R. Holland, "None Were with Him," *Ensign,* May 2009, 87; emphasis in original.
19. Irenaeus, *Against Heresies* IV.xx.6, in *The Early Christian Fathers,* ed. and trans. Henry Bettenson (Oxford: Oxford University Press, 1969), 76.
20. Hebrews 9:15; 12:24; D&C 76:69.
21. Joseph F. Smith, Funeral Sermon preached April 11, 1878, in *Journal of Discourses,* 26 vols., reported by G. D. Watt et al. Liverpool: F.D. and S. W. Richards, et al., 1851–1886 (reprint Salt Lake City: n.p., 1974), 19:264.
22. Cited in Robert Payne, *The Fathers of the Eastern Church* (New York: Dorset, 1985), 17.
23. D&C 76:22–23.
24. D&C 45:2–5.
25. John 14:16, 25–26.
26. John 14:18.
27. Jeffrey R. Holland, *However Long and Hard the Road* (Salt Lake City: Deseret Book, 1985), 47.
28. Johannes Behm, "παράκλητος," *Theological Dictionary of the New Testament,* ed. Gerhard Kittel and Gerhard Friedrich (Grand Rapids, MI: Eerdmans, 1991), 5:803–4.
29. M. Russell Ballard described the plan as "designed by Heavenly Parents who love us" (*When Thou Art Converted: Continuing Our Search for Happiness* [Salt Lake City: Deseret Book, 2001], 62).
30. Genesis 15:12, 17.
31. Hebrews 10:19.
32. Hebrews 10:20.

Chapter 9: The Healing Christ

1. Martin Luther, quoted in Roland Bainton, *Here I Stand: A Life of Martin Luther* (New York: Abingdon, 1950), 65.
2. *The Complete Discourses of Brigham Young,* ed. Richard S. Van Wagoner (Salt Lake City: Smith-Petit Foundation, 2009), 3:1224, 3:1278.
3. Julian of Norwich, *Revelation* XIV, chap. 61 in *The Showings of Julian of Norwich,* ed. Denise M. Baker (New York: W.W. Norton & Co., 2005), 97.
4. Anthony Zimmerman, *Evolution and the Sin in Eden* (New York: University Press of America, 1998), 152–53.
5. Marcellino D'Ambrosio, *Who Were the Church Fathers* (London: SPCK, 2015), 197–98.
6. Charles Hodge, *Systematic Theology* (Grand Rapids, MI: Eerdmans, 1960), 2:192.
7. Gabriel Daly, "Theological Models in the Doctrine of Original Sin," *Heythrop Journal* 13.2 (April 1972): 121.

NOTES

8. 1 Nephi, page 31, 1830 edition (1 Nephi 13:32).
9. See *Analysis of Textual Variants of the Book of Mormon*, ed. Royal Skousen (Provo, UT: Foundation for Ancient Research and Mormon Studies, 2004), 1:290–91. "State of awful wickedness" is in fact the wording found in Skousen's *The Book of Mormon: The Earliest Text* (New Haven, CT: Yale University Press, 2009), 36.
10. Dale G. Renlund, "Our Good Shepherd," *Ensign*, May 2017, 30. He is citing John 10:11, 14; Alma 5:38; D&C 50:44; Isaiah 40:11; Ezekiel 34:16; Isaiah 1:6, 18.
11. Mosiah 3:19.
12. James D. G. Dunn, *The New Perspective on Paul*, rev. ed. (Grand Rapids, MI: Eerdmans, 2008). See his entire work, but the preface especially for a summation.
13. Elizabeth A. Clark, *The Origenist Controversy: The Cultural Construction of an Early Christian Debate* (Princeton, NJ: Princeton University Press, 1992), 250.
14. Krister Stendahl, *Paul Among Jews and Gentiles* (Philadelphia, PA: Fortress Press, 1979), 40–41.
15. Kent L. Yinger, *The New Perspective on Paul: An Introduction* (Eugene, OR: Wipf and Stock, 2011), 23.
16. Ibid., 28.
17. Stendahl, *Paul Among Jews and Gentiles*, 85.
18. *Complete Discourses of Brigham Young*, 4:2020.
19. Peter J. Thuesen, *Predestination: The American Career of a Contentious Doctrine* (New York: Oxford University Press, 2009), 103.
20. Mosiah 27:25.
21. *Complete Discourses of Brigham Young*, 4:2125.
22. Ibid., 2:922.
23. Moses 6:53–55; emphasis added.
24. Dieter F. Uchtdorf, "He Will Place You on His Shoulders and Carry You Home," *Ensign*, May 2016, 104.
25. John Meyendorff, *Byzantine Theology: Historical Trends and Doctrinal Themes* (New York: Fordham University Press, 1999), 145.
26. Theodoret of Cyrus, *In Rom.*, in Meyendorff, *Byzantine Theology*, 145.
27. Meyendorff, *Byzantine Theology*, 145.
28. Joseph Smith, *The Words of Joseph Smith*, eds. Andrew F. Ehat and Lyndon W. Cook (Orem, UT: Grandin Book Company, 1991), 200–201.
29. *Times and Seasons* 2.15 (1 June 1841): 429.
30. Smith, *Words*, 80.
31. Romans 12:21.
32. Alfred, Lord Tennyson, *In Memoriam* LII (New York: Norton, 2004), 38–39.
33. Alexander Elchaninov, *The Diary of a Russian Priest*, trans. Helen Iswolsky (Yonkers, NY: St Vladimir's Seminary Press, 1967), 124.
34. Joseph Smith to the Relief Society, in *The First Fifty Years of Relief Society: Key Documents in Latter-day Saint Women's History*, ed. Jill Mulvay Derr, Carol Cornwall Madsen, Kate Holbrook, and Matthew J. Grow (Salt Lake City: Church Historian's Press, 2016), 78.

Chapter 10: The Collaborative Christ

1. Marilynne Robinson, *Gilead* (New York: Picador, 2004), 124.
2. Martin Luther King, "Letter from a Birmingham Jail," in Patrick Mason, *Planted* (Salt Lake City: Deseret Book, 2015), 112.

NOTES

3. R. L. Richard, "Trinity, Holy," in *New Catholic Encyclopedia*, 15 vols. (New York: McGraw-Hill, 1967), 14:299.
4. Paul Achtemeier, ed., *Harper's Bible Dictionary* (San Francisco: Harper and Row, 1985), 1099. This and the above source are cited in a fuller discussion of the subject by Stephen Robinson, *Are Mormons Christians?* (Salt Lake City: Bookcraft, 1991), 71–89.
5. For an overview of the tradition, see Terryl Givens, *When Souls Had Wings: Pre-Mortal Existence in Western Thought* (New York: Oxford University Press, 2010), 9–17 esp.
6. M. Russell Ballard, "Family Councils," *Ensign*, May 2016, 65.
7. Nikolai Berdyaev, *Destiny of Man* (London: Geoffrey Bles, 1937), 69.
8. See Mosiah 18:8–10.
9. Mosiah 24:13–16. We thank Jacob Rennaker for this insight.
10. Jennifer Reeder and Kate Holbrook, eds., *At the Pulpit: 185 Years of Discourses by Latter-day Saint Women* (Salt Lake City: Church Historian's Press, 2017), 118.
11. Dorothy Sayers, *Meaning of the Creative Act*, 293, in Marie Magdalene Davy, *Nicolas Berdyaev: Man of the Eighth Day* (London: Geoffrey Bles, 1967), 104; Berdyaev, *Destiny of Man*, 138.
12. Berdyaev, *Destiny of Man*, 134–35.
13. Tyler Johnson, "Empathy and the Atonement," *BYU Studies* 55.4 (2016), 110, 117.
14. Spencer W. Kimball, "Small Acts of Service," *Ensign*, December 1974, 5.
15. *The Complete Discourses of Brigham Young*, ed. Richard S. Van Wagoner (Salt Lake City: Smith-Petit Foundation, 2009), 3:1480.
16. John Wesley, "Of Good Angels," *Sermons on Several Occasions* (Nashville: E. Stevenson & F. A. Owen, 1855), 3:206.
17. Recorded by Benjamin Johnson, in Benjamin E. Park, "Early Mormon Patriarchy and the Paradoxes of Democratic Religiosity in Jacksonian America," *American Nineteenth Century History* (2013): 7.
18. Elaine Pagels, *Beyond Belief: The Secret Gospel of Thomas* (New York: Random House, 2003), 10.
19. "Teaching of the Twelve Apostles" IX, in *The Ante-Nicene Fathers*, ed. Alexander Roberts and James Donaldson (Grand Rapids, MI: Eerdmans, 1977), 7:380.
20. D&C 10:52–55.
21. D&C 49:8.
22. Berdyaev, *Creative Act*, 293, in Davy, *Nicolas Berdyaev*, 104.
23. Martin Luther, "The Freedom of a Christian," in Luther, *Selected Writings of Martin Luther*, ed. Theodore G. Tappert (Minneapolis, MN: Fortress Press, 2007), 2:43.
24. Obadiah 1:21.
25. Joseph Smith, in *Times and Seasons* 2.14 (15 May 1841): 430. Smith's revision of the Genesis account of the Abrahamic covenant first appeared in print in *Times and Seasons* 3.9 (1 March 1842): 706 (Abraham 2:11).
26. *Complete Discourses of Brigham Young*, 1:61.
27. Berdyaev, *Destiny of Man*, 138.
28. C. S. Lewis, *The Weight of Glory* (New York: HarperOne, 2015), 46.
29. Parley P. Pratt, "Materiality," *The Prophet* 1.52 (24 May 1845), reprinted in *Millennial Star* 6.2 (1 July 1845): 19–22.

NOTES

30. David G. McAfee, Twitter post retrieved from https://twitter.com/DavidGMcAfee/status/590968327855591424, April 22, 2015.
31. Dietrich von Hildebrand, *The Heart* (South Bend, IN: St. Augustine's Press, 2007), 47.
32. Alisdair MacIntyre, *After Virtue* (Notre Dame, IN: University of Notre Dame Press, 2007), 52–53.
33. See John 10:10.
34. Mark 2:1–5.
35. Mark 2:9.
36. Hannah Givens served in the Peru Lima Mission, 2014–2015.
37. John 15:15.
38. Mark 7:29.
39. John 4:40.
40. Luke 24:28–29.
41. Matthew 8:31–32.
42. 3 Nephi 17:5–7.
43. Gregory of Nazianzus, "Oration 37," in Philip Schaff, ed., *Nicene and Post-Nicene Fathers of the Christian Church*, second series (Peabody, MA: Hendrickson, 1999), 7:338.
44. Justin Martyr, *Second Apology* XII, in *Ante-Nicene Fathers*, 1:192.
45. Moses 7:45.
46. Roger Scruton, *The Face of God* (London: Continuum, 2012), 172–73.
47. A. J. Cronin, *Keys of the Kingdom* (New York: Back Bay Books, 1969), 212.
48. Charles Taylor, *A Secular Age* (Cambridge, MA: Harvard University Press, 2007), 655.
49. Edward Beecher, *The Concord of Ages* (New York: Derby and Jackson, 1860), 98.
50. Scruton, *Face of God*, 176.
51. John Meyendorff, *Byzantine Theology: Historical Trends and Doctrinal Themes* (New York: Fordham University Press, 1999), 201.
52. Ibid., 204.
53. Irenaeus, *Against Heresies* IV.xviii.5, in *Ante-Nicene Fathers*, 1:486.
54. 3 Nephi 18:7.
55. Ibid.

Chapter 11: The Judging Christ

1. D&C 58:42; emphasis added.
2. Wendell Berry, "To My Mother," in *New Collected Poems* (Berkeley: Counterpoint, 2012), 319.
3. Nikolai Berdyaev, *Destiny of Man* (London: Geoffrey Bles, 1937), 139–40.
4. Isaiah 1:18.
5. Morwenna Ludlow, *Universal Salvation* (Oxford: Oxford University Press, 2000), 4.
6. *Dies irae, dies illa/ Solvet saeclum in favilla/ . . . Quantus tremor est futurus/ Quando judex est venturus*. English Translation of Mozart's *Requiem*, http://manlywarringahchoir.org.au/files/2011/01/English-Translation-of-Mozart-Requiem.pdf.
7. John 12:47.
8. Alma 21:17.
9. John 8:10–11.

NOTES

10. See Revelation 12:10.
11. So "Satan" is translated by the New American Standard Bible (Psalm 109:6). It is more often translated as "adversary."
12. Berdyaev, *Destiny of Man*, 140.
13. D&C 121:42.
14. Joseph Smith, *The Words of Joseph Smith*, eds. Andrew F. Ehat and Lyndon W. Cook (Orem, UT: Grandin Book Company, 1991), 80.
15. Berdyaev, *Destiny of Man*, 140.
16. William Shakespeare, *The Merchant of Venice* IV.lll.192–93 (New York: Washington Square Press, 1992), 155.
17. Alma 41:14.
18. Genesis 3:22.
19. Smith, *Words*, 123.
20. Julian of Norwich, *Showing* I, chap. 6 in *Showings*, trans. Edmund Colledge and James Walsh (Mahwah, NJ: Paulist Press, 1978), 186.
21. William Blake, "The Little Black Boy," line 14, in *Songs of Innocence* (1789).
22. Moses 7:41.
23. Romans 8:38–39.
24. John Milton, *Paradise Lost* IV.ll. 52–56 (New York: Penguin, 2000), 75.
25. 1 John 4:19.
26. Exodus 33:12, 17.
27. *Shall We Dance?* dir. Peter Chelsom, Miramax Lionsgate, 2004.
28. Martin Buber, *I and Thou*, trans. Walter Kaufmann (New York: Touchstone, 1996), 78.
29. Charles Darwin, *The Origin of Species* (New York: Bantam, 2008), 186.
30. Mark 10:18–20.
31. Julian of Norwich, *Showing* XVI, chap. 79 in *Showings*, 334. Our re-rendering.
32. Mark 10:21.
33. Julian of Norwich, *Showing* XVI, chap. 76, in *Showings*, 329; *Showing* XVI, chap. 79, 333–34.
34. Marilynne Robinson, *Gilead* (New York: Picador, 2004), 248.
35. These reflections on the rich young man we first presented at an Affirmation conference in Provo, Utah, 30 September 2012. https://www.youtube.com/watch?v=jhTG_-NVTJU. For a similar subsequent treatment, see S. Mark Palmer, "Then Jesus Beholding Him Loved Him," *Ensign*, May 2017, 114–16.
36. 2 Nephi 9:14.
37. C. S. Lewis, *Readings for Meditation and Reflection* (New York: Harper Collins, 1996), 59.
38. 1 Corinthians 13:12.
39. Luke 15:17.
40. Alma 34:34.
41. All these ideas and other parallels are in Emanuel Swedenborg, *Heaven and Hell*, trans. John Ager (Rookhope, UK: Aziloth, 2011).
42. Swedenborg, *Heaven and Hell*, 245.
43. 1 Corinthians 11:32, Young's Literal Translation version.
44. 2 Nephi 9:14.
45. Swedenborg, *Heaven and Hell*, 251.

NOTES

46. Dieter F. Uchtdorf, "O How Great the Plan of Our God!," *Ensign*, November 2016, 21.
47. See 1 Corinthians 13:12.
48. Ether 12:37.
49. William Shakespeare, *Hamlet* III.i.70–71 (New York: Simon & Schuster, 2012), 127; from John Keats to George and Georgiana Keats (14 Feb.–3 May 1819), *The Letters of John Keats* (London: Reeves & Turner, 1895), 304.
50. Irenaeus, *Against Heresies* IV.xxxix.1, in *The Ante-Nicene Fathers*, ed. Alexander Roberts and James Donaldson (Grand Rapids, MI: Eerdmans, 1977), 1:522.
51. James E. Talmage, *The House of the Lord* (Salt Lake City: Deseret Book, 1968), 57, 60.
52. Smith, *Words*, 346.
53. *The Complete Discourses of Brigham Young*, ed. Richard S. Van Wagoner (Salt Lake City: Smith-Petit Foundation, 2009), 2:1132.
54. Charles Penrose, in Conference Report, April 1906, 91.
55. Romans 10:9.
56. Mark 8:23–25.
57. Emily Dickinson, #1129, in *The Complete Poems*, ed. Thomas H. Johnson (Boston: Little, Brown and Co., 1960), 507.
58. Robinson, *Gilead*, 124.
59. See Luke 6:19.

Chapter 12: The Saving Christ

1. Julian of Norwich, *Showings* II and III, chaps. 10 and 11 in *Showings*, trans. Edmund Colledge and James Walsh (Mahwah, NJ: Paulist Press, 1978), 194–95, 199.
2. Joseph Smith, *The Words of Joseph Smith*, eds. Andrew F. Ehat and Lyndon W. Cook (Orem, UT: Grandin Book Company, 1991), 33.
3. Job 38:7; emphasis added.
4. Morwenna Ludlow, *Universal Salvation* (Oxford: Oxford University Press, 2000), 1.
5. Origen, *De Principiis* II.xi.6, in *The Ante-Nicene Fathers*, ed. Alexander Roberts and James Donaldson (Grand Rapids, MI: Eerdmans, 1977), 4:299.
6. Ludlow, *Universal Salvation*, 90n42.
7. Origen, *De Principiis* III.v.8, in *Ante-Nicene Fathers*, 4:344.
8. "Eternal" he interprets as "lasting an age" and not as "lasting forever." B. E. Daley, *The Hope of the Early Church* (Cambridge: Cambridge University Press, 1991), 56, in Ludlow, *Universal Salvation*, 244; D&C 19:10–13.
9. Daley, *Hope of the Early Church*, 58, in Ludlow, *Universal Salvation*, 36.
10. Ludlow, *Universal Salvation*, 1–2.
11. Clementine, *Recognitions* 1.lii, in *Ante-Nicene Fathers*, 8:91.
12. Catholicism has since expressed recurrently a softening of this position, notably in John Paul II's *Redemptoris Missio*: "The universality of salvation means that it is granted not only to those who explicitly believe in Christ and have entered the Church. Since salvation is offered to all, it must be made concretely available to all" (http://w2.vatican.va/content/john-paul-ii/en/encyclicals/documents/hf_jp-ii_enc_07121990_redemptoris-missio.html). Jesuit theologian Karl Rahner, with his notion of the "anonymous Christian," holds that "a person

NOTES

lives in the grace of God and attains salvation outside of explicitly constituted Christianity ... because he follows his conscience" (in *Dialogue: Conversations and Interviews, 1965–82,* ed. Paul Imhof and Hubert Biallowons [New York: Crossroad, 1986], 207).

13. "Blessing by Joseph Smith Sr. Dated December 9, 1834," *Early Patriarchal Blessings of The Church of Jesus Christ of Latter-day Saints,* comp. H. Michael Marquardt (Salt Lake City: Smith-Pettit Foundation, 2007), 11.
14. Lavina Fielding Anderson, ed., *Lucy's Book: A Critical Edition of Lucy Mack Smith's Family Memoir* (Salt Lake City: Signature Books, 2001), 73.
15. Dean C. Jessee, ed., *The Papers of Joseph Smith, Volume 1: Autobiographical and Historical Writings* (Salt Lake City: Deseret Book, 1989), 2:440; Smith, Words, 112.
16. Smith, *Words,* 318.
17. Revelation 21:4.
18. Joseph Smith, Manuscript History of the Church, E-1, 1681. In Church History Library.
19. Emma took "Freedom of the Will" from an 1805 camp-meeting collection. Michael Hicks, *Music and Mormonism: A History* (Urbana: University of Illinois Press, 1989), 21.
20. 2 Nephi 28:8.
21. D&C 121:41–42.
22. 2 Peter 3:9.
23. Isaiah 49:16.
24. Hebrews 13:5.
25. C. S. Lewis, *The Joyful Christian* (New York: Simon & Schuster, 1996), 77–78.
26. Matthew 5:48.
27. See Smith, *Words,* 351.
28. Ἔσεσθε οὖν ὑμεῖς τέλειοι, or "Therefore you shall be whole, complete."
29. David A. Bednar, "Faithful Parents and Wayward Children: Sustaining Hope While Overcoming Misunderstanding," *Ensign,* March 2014, 31.
30. John 12:32; emphasis added.
31. Colossians 1:17, New Revised Standard Version.
32. Romans 14:11.
33. 2 Nephi 26:24.
34. 3 Nephi 27:14.
35. 2 Nephi 2:27.
36. Dietrich Bonhoeffer to Eberhard Bethge, 16 July 1944, in Larry L. Rasmussen, *Dietrich Bonhoeffer: Reality and Resistance* (Louisville: John Knox, 2005), 83.
37. D&C 121:46.
38. Mark 15:39. See also Matthew 27:54; Luke 23:47.
39. Dorothy Sayers, *The Mind of the Maker* (London: Methuen, 1941), 110.
40. Dieter F. Uchtdorf, "The Gift of Grace," *Ensign,* May 2015, 107–10.
41. Dieter F. Uchtdorf, "He Will Place You on His Shoulders and Carry You Home," *Ensign,* May 2016, 101–4.
42. Nikolai Berdyaev, *Destiny of Man* (London: Geoffrey Bles, 1937), 138.
43. Kenneth E. Kirk, *Vision of God* (New York: Harper & Row, 1966), 132–33.
44. Romans 12:2, New Revised Standard Version.
45. Genesis 3:6.

NOTES

46. Dallin H. Oaks, "Fundamental Premises of Our Faith," *Deseret News*, http://www.deseretnews.com/media/pdf/24370.pdf.
47. Moses 7:32–33.
48. Job 35:6–7.
49. Paul Ricoeur, "On Accusation," in Alisdair MacIntyre and Paul Ricoeur, *The Religious Significance of Atheism* (New York: Columbia University Press, 1970), 68.
50. B. H. Roberts, *The Life of John Taylor* (Salt Lake City: G. Q. Cannon, 1892), 424.
51. Manuscript History of the Church, D-1, 1387, addenda.
52. Peter Hobbs, *The Short Day Dying* (New York: Harcourt, 2005), 18.
53. Edward Farley, "A Missing Presence," *The Christian Century* (March 18–25, 1998): 276.
54. William Shakespeare, Sonnet 116.
55. Alexander Galbraith, *Human Creeds and Confessions* (Glasgow: R. Chapman, 1822), 9–10.
56. Karen Lynn Davidson, "O Savior, Thou Who Wearest a Crown," *Hymns of The Church of Jesus Christ of Latter-day Saints* (1985), no. 197.
57. Manuscript History of the Church, D-1, 1387, addenda.
58. Parley Pratt presided over the Church court of some such members (see Terryl Givens and Mathew Grow, *Parley Pratt: The Apostle Paul of Mormonism* [New York: Oxford University Press, 2011], 67); Warren Foote recorded that "[Ezra] Landon and others had been cut off for rejecting concerning the three glories" (*Autobiography of Warren Foote* [Mesa, AZ: Dale Arnold Foote, 1997], 1:5).
59. D&C 88:32.
60. John Smith, "True Way or Method of Attaining to Divine Knowledge," in C. A. Patrides, ed. *The Cambridge Platonists* (London: Edward Arnold, 1969), 129.
61. Francis Fukuyama, *The Origins of Political Order* (New York: Farrar, Straus, and Giroux, 2011), 41.
62. Aquinas, *Summa Theologica*, Suppl. Tertia Partis, Q 94 Art 1 (New York: Benziger Brothers, 1948), 3:2972.
63. William Dawes, *Eternity of Hell Torments* (London, 1707), 11, in John Casey, *After Lives: A Guide to Heaven, Hell, and Purgatory* (New York: Oxford University Press, 2009), 216.
64. This was John Murray's characterization of contemporary Christianity, in *Letters and Sketches of Sermons* (Boston: Joshua Belcher, 1812), 2:39.
65. Luke 15:30.
66. Matthew 20:12.
67. D&C 117:11.
68. Jonah 3:4.
69. Jonah 3:10.
70. Moses 7:41.
71. Jonah 4:11.
72. Franklin D. Richards, "Words of the Prophets," Church History Library; Charlotte Haven, 26 March 1843, "A Girl's Letters from Nauvoo," *The Overland Monthly* 16.96 (December1890): 626, http://www.olivercowdery.com/smithhome/1880s-1890s/havn1890.htm. I thank Michael Reed for these sources.
73. *Wilford Woodruff's Journal*, ed. Scott G. Kenney (Midvale: Signature Books, 1983), 4:334.

NOTES

74. Lorenzo Snow, "Preaching the Gospel in the Spirit World," *Collected Discourses*, ed. Brian Stuy (n.p.:B. H. S. Publishing, 1989), 3:364.
75. Brigham Henry Roberts, *Outlines of Ecclesiastical History: A Textbook* (Salt Lake City: Cannon & Sons, 1893), 427.
76. James E. Talmage, *Articles of Faith* (Salt Lake City: Deseret News, 1899), 421.
77. James E. Talmage, in Conference Report, April 1930, 98.
78. Joseph F. Smith, Funeral Sermon preached April 11, 1878, in *Journal of Discourses*, 26 vols., reported by G. D. Watt et al. (Liverpool: F.D. and S. W. Richards, et al., 1851–1886); reprint (Salt Lake City: n.p., 1974,) 19:264.
79. J. Reuben Clark Jr., in *Church News*, 23 April 1960, 3.
80. See Alma 1:1–4.
81. D&C 88:34.
82. See Alma 11:34–37.
83. Alma 34:34.
84. "That same spirit which doth possess your bodies at the time that ye go out of this life, that same spirit will have power to possess your body in that eternal world" (Alma 34:34).
85. D&C 98:3.
86. Christopher Marlowe, *The Tragical History of Doctor Faustus*, in *Works*, ed. A. H. Bullen (London: Nimmo, 1885), 1:272.
87. Alma 41:10.
88. Mosiah 2:41.
89. 2 Nephi 9:50.
90. Smith, *Words*, 358.
91. Letter from the Office of The First Presidency, 5 March 1952, and again on 17 December 1965. Cited in George T. Boyd, "A Mormon Concept of Man," *Dialogue* 3.1 (Spring 1968):72.
92. D&C 76:112.
93. Moses 7:35.
94. D&C 19:6–7.
95. Sasse, "αἰών," *Theological Dictionary of the New Testament*, ed. Gerhard Kittel and Gerhard Friedrich (Grand Rapids, MI: Eerdmans, 1991), 1:198–99.
96. D&C 76:72, 74.
97. D&C 137:6.
98. James E. Faust, "Dear Are the Sheep That Have Wandered," *Ensign*, May 2003, 61.
99. Robert D. Hales, in North America Northeast Area Broadcast, 26 April 2015.
100. Hebrews 13:5.
101. Romans 8:38–39.
102. George Q. Cannon, "Remarks," *Deseret Evening News*, March 7, 1891, 4.
103. Boyd K. Packer, "The Brilliant Morning of Forgiveness," *Ensign*, November 1995, 20.
104. Jeffrey R. Holland, "The Laborers in the Vineyard," *Ensign*, May 2012, 33.
105. Ephesians 3:18.
106. C. S. Lewis, *The Letters of C. S. Lewis*, ed. W. H. Lewis and Walter Hooper (New York: HarperCollins, 1993), 418.
107. Kirk, *Vision of God*, 343–44.
108. Origen, *Against Celsus*, VIII.lxxii, in *Ante-Nicene Fathers*, 4:667.

NOTES

109. Antonia Tripolitis, *The Doctrine of the Soul in the Thought of Plotinus and Origen* (Roslyn Heights, NY: Libra, 1978), 114.
110. Thomas Traherne, *Selected Writings*, ed. Dick Davis (Manchester: Carcanet, 1980), 84.
111. Macrina the Younger, *De Anima et Resurrection*, 8, in Robert Payne, *The Fathers of the Eastern Church* (New York: Dorset, 1985), 162.
112. 2 Nephi 26:24; emphasis added.
113. Enos 1:7.
114. Julian of Norwich, *Showing* XIII, chap. 32 in *Showings*, 233.
115. Alma 5:37; emphasis added.

Epilogue

1. Gerard Manley Hopkins, "On the Portrait of Two Beautiful Young People," *The Major Works* (New York: Oxford University Press, 2009), 176.
2. Robinson Jeffers, "The Epic Stars," in *The Selected Poetry*, ed. Tim Hunt (Stanford: Stanford University Press, 2002), 699.
3. Mark Helprin, "Falling into Eternity," *First Things*, March 2017.
4. Genesis 3:22.
5. 1 Corinthians 13:8.
6. Helaman 5:12.
7. 1 Nephi 11:8.
8. 1 Nephi 11:15.
9. 1 Nephi 11:21–22.
10. Robert Bolt, *A Man for All Seasons* (New York: Methuen, 1988), 88.
11. John Keats, *Poetical Works and Letters* (Boston: Houghton Mifflin, 1899), 39.
12. The original words are often attributed to Teresa de Avila: *"No me mueve, mi Dios para quererte, el cielo que me tienes prometido, ni me mueve el infierno tan temido para dejar por eso de ofenderte. . . . Muéveme, al fin, tu amor de tal manera que aunque no hubiera cielo, yo te amara y aunque no hubiera infierno, te temiera,"* in *Luz de verdades católicas* (Barcelona: Rafael Figueró, 1705), 336.

INDEX

Abraham, 60
Accountability, 54–56
Accusatory judgment, 92–93
Adam: language of, 4; clothing of, 51–52; shame of, 90. *See also* Fall
Adoption, 48–52, 74–75
Advocate, 58–60. *See also* Mediator(s) and mediation
Afflictions, 35–36, 127–29. *See also* Opposition
Agency, 33–36, 38, 54–56, 93, 107, 108–10. *See also* Choice; Self-determination
Ambrose, 22
Aquinas, Thomas, 116
Aristotle, 81
Arminianism, 35
Asay, Carlos E., 52
Assyria, 117–18
Atonement, 53–62, 74
Augustine, xi–xii, 22, 29–30, 34, 39, 105

Ballard, M. Russell, 74
Baptism, 50–52, 74–75
Baptism for the dead, 106
Bednar, David A., 108–9
Beecher, Edward, xvii, 6, 88
Beliefs, significance of, 6
ben Israel, Menasseh, 12–13
Berdyaev, Nikolai, xvii, 31, 75, 80, 91–92, 93, 110–11
Berry, Wendell, 91
Bible, loss of plain and precious things from, 5
Blake, William, 94
Body, divinity of, 28–29
Bonhoeffer, Dietrich, 109
Book of Mormon, 65–67
Bourguet, Daniel, 17
Buber, Martin, 96
Burdens, bearing one another's, 74–79
Burton, Theodore M., 47
Byron, George Gordon, Lord, 37

153

INDEX

Calvin, John, xvi, 23, 34, 35, 40
Cannon, George Q., 124
Celsus, 17–18
Children, wayward, 108–9, 118, 123–24
Children of God, 11–12, 48–49
Choice, 31, 54–56. *See also* Agency
Christians, finding shared ground with fellow, 1–2
Chrysostom, John, 33
Church Fathers, x–xv; Ignatius, x, 50, 58, 89; Justin Martyr, x, 17, 87; Polycarp, x–xi; Tertullian, x–xi, 1, 19, 29, 37, 46, 78; Augustine, xi–xii, 22, 29–30, 34, 39, 105; Clement of Alexandria, xii, 19, 29; Pelagius, xii, 33–34; Macrina, xiii–xiv, 126; Gregory of Nazianzus, xiv, 65, 86–87; Gregory of Nyssa, xiv–xv, 28, 56, 88, 104. *See also* Irenaeus; Origen
Church of Jesus Christ of Latter-day Saints, The: and finding shared ground with other Christians, 1–2; theology of, 2–3
Clark, J. Reuben Jr., 119
Clement of Alexandria, xii, 19, 29
Clothing, sacred, 51–52
Collaboration, 73–89
Collection of English Prose and Verse, 24–25
Comforter, 59–60
Comforting others, 74–79
Commandments, 112–13
Comparison, 114–16
Compassion, 74–79, 85–86, 94
Condemnation, 92–93, 100
Confession of Faith, 21
Consequences, 54–56
Council in heaven, 11–12, 48
Creeds, 24
Cronin, A. J., 87

Darwin, Charles, 96
Dawes, William, 116
Day of Judgment, 100
Dead, redemption of, 79–80, 106
Death: introduced into world, 26–27, 37–38; possibility of repentance after, 101; progression following, 118–19

Decision making, 31
Degrees of glory, 118–23. *See also* Heaven
Deification, 46–47, 49, 80, 112. *See also* Divine nature
Discipleship: compassion in, 74–79, 94; and self-perception, 99
Disease, 66
Disobedience, 101
Divine nature: of Jesus Christ, 17–18; of man, 28–29. *See also* Deification
Dream, of Jesus Christ, 76–77

Eastern Church, ix, 9, 37, 38, 39
Eastern Fathers: Ignatius, x, 50, 58, 89; Polycarp, x–xi; Clement of Alexandria, xii, 19, 29; Macrina, xiii–xiv, 126; Gregory of Nazianzus, xiv, 65, 86–87; Gregory of Nyssa, xiv–xv, 28, 56, 88, 104. *See also* Irenaeus; Origen
Eckhart, Meister, 39
Edwards, Jonathan, 46
Elihu, 112
Enoch, 94
Erasmus, 23
"Eternal," 122
Eternal life, 47, 50, 56–57
Eternal progression, 104, 121. *See also* Spiritual progression
Eternal punishment, 122
Ethics, 81–82
Eucharist, 50, 87, 88–89
Eve: and effects of Fall, 16; clothing of, 51–52; shame of, 90. *See also* Fall
Evil, 45–46
Exaltation: Clement of Alexandria on, xii; through plan of salvation, 11–12; Fall and, 28; agency and, 35–36
Eye, 96

Fairness, 115–16, 118
Faith: Luther on, xvi; through trials, 127–29
Fall: loss of understanding of, 14–16; pre-Restoration teachings on, 26–32, 41–42; sin and, 37–40; in plan of

INDEX

salvation, 41; and human nature, 69–72; judgment and, 94

Family: shame and, 90–91; salvation with, 106–7. *See also* Relationships

Farley, Edward, 113

Fatherhood, of God, 18–21, 48–49; of Jesus Christ, 48–51

Faust, James E., 123

Flake, Kathleen, 89

Forgetting of sins, 91–92

Forgiveness, 84, 91–92, 93–94

Formula of Concord, 39

Frost, Robert, 13

Fukuyama, Francis, 114

Galbraith, Alexander, 113

Garment, 52

Gifts of the Spirit, 129

God: and limitations of language, 4–5; character of, 6, 113; children of, 11–12, 48–49; nature of, 17–25, 36, 107–8; will of, 23–24, 112; agency and omnipotence of, 35; glory of, 46; entering presence of, 61; in Godhead, 74; love of, 94–95, 98, 124–25

Goddard, Emma N., 75

Godhead, 17–18, 73–74

Golden Rule, 80–81

Good: seeking after, 1–2; impact of, 72

Good works, 110–11

Grace, xvi, 11–12

Gregory of Nazianzus, xiv, 65, 86–87

Gregory of Nyssa, xiv–xv, 28, 56, 88, 104

Gregory Palamas, 29

Guilt, 67–68

Hales, Robert D., 124

Happiness, 81–82, 84–85, 102, 112–13, 114–16

Haven, Charlotte, 118

Healing, 63–72, 76–77, 82–87, 92, 101–2

Heaven, 74, 78, 106–7, 118–23

Hell, 105, 116

Helprin, Mark, 128

Hilary of Poitiers, 22

Hildebrand, Dietrich von, 81

Hodge, Charles, 65

Holland, Jeffrey R., 57, 59–60, 124

Holy Ghost, 59–60, 74

Hopkins, Gerard Manley, 127

Human eye, 96

Human nature, 67, 68–72

Ignatius, x, 50, 58, 89

Illness, 82–84

Immortality, 56–57

Interconnectedness, 74–79

Intimacy, shame and, 90–91

Irenaeus: life of, xi; on God and creation, 20; on nature of God, 20, 46; on Fall, 26, 27, 28, 29; on agency, 33, 38; on becoming perfected, 41; on Atonement, 57; on Eucharist, 88; on obedience and disobedience, 101

Jeffers, Robinson, 127

Jesus Christ: joint-heirship with, xiii; Restoration and understanding of, 1, 2–3, 43–44; divinity of, 17–18; and divide between God and man, 20, 22–23; worshipped by Latter-day Saints, 43; selflessness of, 45–47; adoption by, 48–52; Atonement of, 53–62, 74; healing through, 63–72; collaboration with, 73–89; role of, in Godhead, 74; trauma victim's dream of, 76–77; judgment and, 90–102; love of, 97–98, 113–14, 131; building foundation on, 130

John Paul II, Pope, 54

Johnson, Tyler, 77

Joint-heirship with Christ, xiii

Jonah, 117–18

Judaism, teachings on preexistence in, 12–13

Judgment, 90–102

Julian of Norwich: life of, xvi–xvii; on Fall, 30–31; on sin, 38; on healing power of Christ, 64; on love of Jesus Christ, 94, 97, 98; on salvation, 103

Justice, 54–56, 115–16, 118

Justin Martyr, x, 17, 87

Kasper, Cardinal Walter, 49

Keats, John, 130–31

INDEX

Keys of the Kingdom, The (Cronin), 87
Kimball, Spencer W., 77
Kindness, 72
King, Martin Luther, 73
Kirk, Kenneth, 124–25

Language, limitations of, 4–7
Levenson, Jon, 13
Lewis, C. S., 36, 80, 99, 124
Lord's Prayer, 19
Lord's Supper, 50, 87, 88–89
Love: impact of, 72; of God, 94–95, 98, 124–25; of Jesus Christ, 97–98, 113–14, 131; noncoercive, 109; works and, 111
Loved ones: shame and, 90–91; salvation with, 106–7. *See also* Relationships
Ludlow, Morwenna, 103–4, 105
Luther, Martin: life of, xvi; on nature of God, 23; on agency, 34–35; on sin, 39, 40; and Protestant Reformation, 63–64; on interconnectedness, 79

MacIntyre, Alisdair, 81–82
Macrina, xiii–xiv, 126
Marriage, 12, 95
Maxwell, Neal A., 40–41
Mediator(s) and mediation, 53, 57–59
Memory, of sin, 91–92
Mercy, 93
Meyendorff, John, 70–71
Mill, John Stuart, 54
Milton, John, 22–23, 41, 95
Missionaries, find woman in need of healing, 85
Monotheism, 18
Mortality: in plan of salvation, 29; trials of, 35–36, 127–29; as effect of Fall, 37–38; purpose of, 47, 100–101, 111–12; agency in, 54–56; sinfulness in, 70–71; early Christian understanding of, 104; as time to repent, 120–21
Mourning with those who mourn, 74–79

Natural man, 67, 68–70
Neighbor, caring for, 74–79
Nephi, vision of, 129–30

New and everlasting covenant, 48. *See also* Plan of salvation
Nietzsche, Friedrich, 112
Nineveh, 117–18
Noncoercive love, 109

Oaks, Dallin H., 112
Obedience, 101, 110
O'Connell, Robert, 34
Old Testament sacrifices, 60–61
Olson, Roger, 18, 23, 49
Opposition, 55–56. *See also* Trials
Ordinances, 112–13
Origen: life of, xii–xiii; on plan of salvation, 13; on separate natures of God and Jesus Christ, 18; on nature of God, 21, 46; on Fall, 28; on mortality, 104; on salvation, 104
Original Church, alteration of teachings of, 9–10
Original sin, x–xi, 39–40, 65, 70

Packer, Boyd K., 124
Pain, 67–68
Paraclete, 59–60
Paralytic, lowered through roof, 82–84
Passions, 70
Paul, 67–68, 71, 94–95
Payne, Robert, 28
Pelagius, xii, 33–34
Penrose, Charles, 101
Perfection, 108
Peru, missionaries in, 85
Pettiness, 116
Philo of Alexandria, 26
Photios, 34
Plan of salvation: alteration of teachings on, 9–10; grace enters universe through, 11–12; set forth in preexistence, 12–14, 48; loss of understanding of, 14–15; Fall's place in, 16, 28, 41; establishment and purpose of, 41
Plato, 47
Polycarp, x–xi
Pratt, Parley P., 80
Predestination, 34–35
Preexistence: Clement of Alexandria

INDEX

on, xii; teachings on, 11–14, 41–42; abandonment of doctrine of, 15; plan of salvation set forth in, 48
Priesthood, 15
Protestant Reformation, 63–64
Punishment, eternal, 122

Redemption of dead, 79–80, 106
Reformation, 63–64
Reformers, xvi, 23–25. *See also* Calvin, John; Luther, Martin
Relationships, 90–91, 95–96. *See also* Family; Loved ones
Renlund, Dale G., 66
Repentance, 70, 91–92, 101, 111–12, 120–21, 123–24
Restoration: and understanding of Jesus Christ, 2–3, 43–44; purpose of, 15; as gathering together of church, 78–79
Resurrection, 29, 37–38, 58, 106
Reward, 115–16, 118
Rich young man, 96–97
Ricoeur, Paul, 36, 112
Roberts, B. H., 50, 54, 118
Robinson, Marilynne, 73, 102
Roman Empire, division of, ix
Roof, paralytic lowered through, 82–84

Sacrament, 50, 87, 88–89
Sacrifices, 60–61
St. Priscilla catacombs, 129
Salvans, 65
Salvation: Luther on, xvi; agency and, 34–36, 107, 108–10; as incorporation into heavenly family, 49–50; forgiveness and, 93–94; early Christian understanding of, 103–5; change in understanding of, 105–6; with loved ones, 106–7; and nature of God, 107–8; and eternal progression, 118–23. *See also* Plan of salvation
Sanctification, 78, 86–89
Sanders, John, 20–21
Satan, 56–57, 71, 93, 95
Sayers, Dorothy, 110
Secular Age, 127–28

Self-determination, 45–46. *See also* Agency
Self-forgiveness, 94
Self-knowledge, 98–100
Selflessness, of Jesus Christ, 45–47
Self-worth, 95–96
Shame, 90–91
Shared suffering, 74–79
Sickness, 82–84
Sin: original sin, x–xi, 39–40, 65, 70; Fall and, 37–41; remission of, 50; human susceptibility to, 69–72; and reparative suffering, 87; forgiveness and forgetting of, 91–92; as pain, 102
Small-heartedness, 116
Smith, Alvin, 105–6, 122–23
Smith, Joseph: on embracing truth, 2; and limitations of language, 4–6; on original Church, 9–10; on council in heaven, 11, 48; on preexistence, 13; on God's omnipotence, 35; on fundamental principles of Mormonism, 43; on purpose of mortality, 47; on baptism, 50; on Atonement, 58; on human nature, 71; on kindness and love, 72; on pure knowledge, 93; on compassion, 94; on repentance after death, 101; on salvation, 103; and death of Alvin Smith, 105–6; on resurrection, 106; on commandments and ordinances, 112–13
Smith, Joseph F., 58, 119
Snow, Erastus, 11
Snow, Lorenzo, 118, 119
Sodzo, 64, 65
Song of the Pearl, 13–14
Sovereignty, 20–25, 35
Spiritual gifts, 129
Spiritual progression, 46–47, 49, 80, 118–23. *See also* Eternal progression
Status, 114, 116
Stendahl, Krister, 67–68
Suffering: of God, 21; shared, 74–79; alleviation of, 85–86; sanctification of, 86–89
Swedenborg, Emanuel, 99, 100
Synergism, 23

INDEX

Talmage, James E., 101, 119, 120
Taylor, Charles, 87, 127
Taylor, John, 112
Temple, 60, 61–62
Temple garment, 52
Temple veil, 61
Tennyson, Alfred, Lord, 72
Terrestrial world, 122
Tertullian, x–xi, 1, 19, 29, 37, 46, 78
Theodore of Mopsuestia, 22, 70
Theodoret of Cyrus, 50, 52, 70
Theophilus of Antioch, 28
Theosis, 46–47, 49, 80, 112. *See also* Divine nature
Traherne, Thomas, 31, 125
Trauma, 76–77
Tree of Life, 129–30
Trials, 35–36, 127–29. *See also* Opposition
Trinity, 73
Truth, embracing, 1–2

Uchtdorf, Dieter F.: on beliefs, 6; on mortality, 70; on Day of Judgment, 100; on salvation, 110
Universal Church, 1–2
Universal Declaration of Human Rights (1948), 45

Vicarious redemption, 79–80
Virtue, 102

Vision, of Julian of Norwich, 30–31
Von Hildebrand, Dietrich, 81

Watson, Thomas, 46
Wayward children, 108–9, 118, 123–24
Weakness, 67–68
Wesley, John, 77–78, 79
Western Church, ix, 9, 39
Western Fathers: Justin Martyr, x, 17, 87; Tertullian, x–xi, 1, 19, 29, 37, 46, 78; Augustine, xi–xii, 22, 29–30, 34, 39, 105; Pelagius, xii, 33–34
Western Reformers, xvi, 23–25. *See also* Calvin, John; Luther, Martin
Westminster Confession, 21, 24
Widtsoe, John, 31
Will of God, 23–24, 112
Works, 110–11
Wright, N. T., 68

Young, Brigham: on God's communication methods, 5; on purpose of mortality, 47; on intention of Saints, 64; on natural man, 68–70; on John Wesley, 77; on death, 101; on postmortal progression, 118

Zero-sum game, 114
Zimmerman, Anthony, 30, 65
Zion-building, 78, 79